D0501680

Copyright © 2014 National Geographic Society

All rights reserved. Reproduction of the whole or any part of the contents without written permission from the publisher is prohibited.

Published by the National Geographic Society
Gary E. Knell, *President and Chief Executive Officer*
John M. Fahey, *Chairman of the Board*
Declan Moore, *Executive Vice President; President, Publishing and Travel*
Melina Gerosa Bellows, *Publisher; Chief Creative Officer, Books, Kids, and Family*

Prepared by the Book Division
Hector Sierra, *Senior Vice President and General Manager*
Nancy Laties Feresten, *Senior Vice President, Kids Publishing and Media*
Jennifer Emmett, *Vice President, Editorial Director, Kids Books*
Eva Absher-Schantz, *Design Director, Kids Publishing and Media*
Jay Sumner, *Director of Photography, Kids Publishing*
R. Gary Colbert, *Production Director*
Jennifer A. Thornton, *Director of Managing Editorial*

Staff for This Book
Priyanka Lamichhane and Marfé Ferguson Delano, *Project Editors*
Kathryn Robbins, *Associate Designer*
Kelley Miller, *Senior Photo Editor*
Ariane Szu-Tu, *Editorial Assistant*
Callie Broaddus, *Design Production Assistant*
Margaret Leist, *Photo Assistant*
Carl Mehler, *Director of Maps*
Grace Hill, *Associate Managing Editor*
Mike O'Connor, *Production Editor*
Lewis R. Bassford, *Production Manager*
Susan Borke, *Legal and Business Affairs*

Production Services
Phillip L. Schlosser, *Senior Vice President*
Chris Brown, *Vice President, NG Book Manufacturing*
George Bounelis, *Senior Production Manager*
Nicole Elliott, *Director of Production*
Rachel Faulise, *Manager*
Robert L. Barr, *Manager*

The National Geographic Society is one of the world's largest nonprofit scientific and educational organizations. Founded in 1888 to "increase and diffuse geographic knowledge," the Society's mission is to inspire people to care about the planet. It reaches more than 400 million people worldwide each month through its official journal, *National Geographic*, and other magazines; National Geographic Channel; television documentaries; music; radio; films; books; DVDs; maps; exhibitions; live events; school publishing programs; interactive media; and merchandise. National Geographic has funded more than 10,000 scientific research, conservation and exploration projects and supports an education program promoting geographic literacy.

For more information, please visit national geographic.com, call 1-800-NGS LINE (647-5463), or write to the following address:
National Geographic Society
1145 17th Street N.W.
Washington, D.C. 20036-4688 U.S.A.

Visit us online at nationalgeographic.com/books

For librarians and teachers: ngchildrensbooks.org

National Geographic supports K-12 educators with ELA Common Core Resources, Visit natgeo.ed/commoncore for more information.

More for kids from National Geographic:
kids.nationalgeographic.com

For information about special discounts for bulk purchases, please contact National Geographic Books Special Sales: ngspecsales@ngs.org

For rights or permissions inquiries, please contact National Geographic Books Subsidiary Rights: ngbookrights@ngs.org

Trade paperback ISBN: 978-1-4263-1484-1
Library edition ISBN: 978-1-4263-1485-8

Printed in the United States of America
14/QGT-CML/1

NATIONAL GEOGRAPHIC KiDS

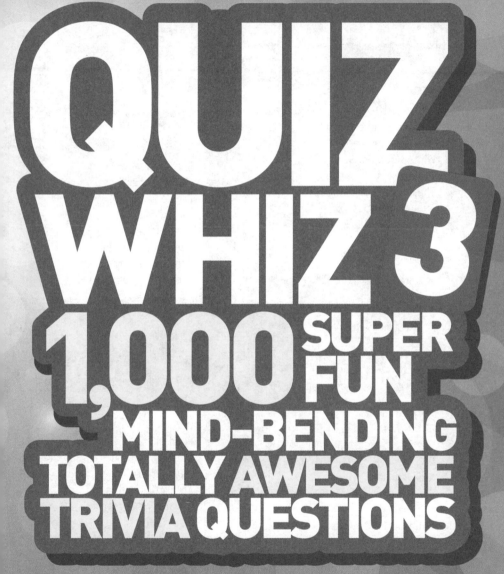

QUIZ WHIZ 3

1,000 SUPER FUN MIND-BENDING TOTALLY AWESOME TRIVIA QUESTIONS

NATIONAL GEOGRAPHIC

WASHINGTON, D.C.

Table of CONTENTS

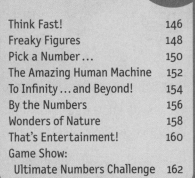

INTRODUCTION

Are you a titan of trivia?

Are you into totally awesome, amazing facts? Then you're in the right place! Welcome to *Quiz Whiz 3*, a treasure trove of fascinating and funny questions.

This continent-skipping collection of curiosities will stretch your smarts and make you giggle with glee. You will learn about the world's fastest roller coaster, India's hottest chili pepper, and the blobfish's claim to fame. You'll learn about some pretty incredible critters, too—a water-skiing rodent, an animal that can live both at the Equator and the Antarctic, and Facebook star Giant George.

Quiz Whiz 3 has 1,000 facts about the gross, the great, and the gigantic. Do you know what type of food features squid ink? Can you guess what type of seafood is found in vending machines in China? Do you know what a group of kangaroos is called? Who was the first Olympic champion on record? You'll learn all this and more in these mind-bending, fact-filled pages.

To take the *Quiz Whiz 3* challenge, you can focus on your favorite topics or tackle them in order. In the "True or False?" quizzes, guess whether the 30 theme-related statements are fact or fiction. Then flip to the answer pages to discover how good your guesses were. In "Map Mania!" quizzes, use maps to locate the places where important inventions originated, where your favorite foods were first feasted on, and where the world's most famous sports arenas are. Multiple-choice questions throughout the book cover sports stars who became celebrities, wacky clothing fads, weird pet facts, and the fastest, smallest, oldest, ugliest, and oddest things on the planet. Each chapter ends with a "Game Show," where you'll find special photo questions and an extra-challenging "Ultimate Brain Buster" question.

If any of the questions send your brain into overload, have no fear. Answers to all of the *Quiz Whiz 3* questions are listed at the end of the book, along with explanations that are sometimes pretty wacky themselves. Tally your correct answers to find out how well you withstood the challenge.

No matter how many questions you conquer, chances are you'll discover topics you want to explore further. The best part of this book is it doesn't matter if anyone gets the answers right.

The reward is in the challenge. Ready? It's time to conquer *Quiz Whiz 3*!

Pet Pals

YOU'VE GOTTA BE KITTEN ME!

1 How many whiskers does the average cat have on each side of its face?

a. 1
b. 3
c. 12
d. 5,007

2 **True or false?** The average cat can spend two-thirds of its life sleeping.

3 When does a cat purr?

a. when it cares for its kittens
b. when it needs comfort
c. when it feels content
d. all of the above

4 What is the average number of kittens in a litter?

a. 1 to 2
b. 4 to 6
c. 8 to 10
d. 12 to 14

5 What was the name of the very first cartoon cat?

a. Caveman Cat
b. Tom (of *Tom and Jerry*)
c. Felix the Cat
d. Garfield

6 Which part of a cat's body can it make appear and disappear?

a. its claws
b. its eyes
c. its whiskers
d. its tail

7 What was the punishment for anyone who killed a cat in ancient Egypt?
a. nine lashes with a cattail
b. death
c. nine days in the stockade
d. exile from the country

8 A cat named Tommaso inherited this much money from his owner when she passed away.
a. $2
b. $20
c. $5,000
d. $13 million

9 Which part of a cat is as unique as a human fingerprint?
a. nose pad
b. paw pads
c. tongue
d. claws

10 Which of these great scientists was known to have cut holes in a door to let cats in and out of the home?
a. Marie Curie
b. Rachel Carson
c. Sir Isaac Newton
d. Bill Nye the Science Guy

11 Which smell is so gross to cats that they will stay away from it?
a. catnip
b. human sweat
c. dog breath
d. orange scent

12 A cat cannot taste _____ flavors.
a. salty
b. sweet
c. bitter
d. sour

A TABBY KITTEN

CHECK YOUR ANSWERS ON PAGES 164–165.

Doggone FUN!

1 The smallest adult dog on record was a member of which breed?
a. poodle
b. Chihuahua
c. Newfoundland
d. miniature schnauzer

2 **True or false?** Dalmatian puppies are born with all the spots they will ever have.

3 **True or false?** Almost all adult dogs have about 320 bones and 42 permanent teeth.

TEACUP POODLE

4 What percentage of dog owners have admitted to signing their pets' names on greeting cards sent from the family?
a. 91 percent
b. 12 percent
c. 2 percent
d. Zero...that's ridiculous!

5 The African basenji is also called the barkless dog. What does this dog do instead of barking?
a. It hums.
b. It uses sign language.
c. It yodels.
d. It doesn't make a sound.

AFRICAN BASENJI

6 About how long does it take to train a Seeing Eye dog?
a. 3 days
b. 2 weeks
c. 4 months
d. 36 months

12

7 Which country has the highest dog population?
a. Venezuela
b. Egypt
c. France
d. the United States

8 Which are the most popular names for male dogs in English-speaking countries?
a. Rover and Fido
b. Phineas and Ferb
c. Max and Buddy
d. Batman and Robin

9 Giant George has his own Facebook page and had a book written about him. What made Giant George so famous?
a. He was the world's shortest dog.
b. He was the world's fastest dog.
c. He was the world's tallest dog.
d. He could update his own Facebook page.

GIANT GEORGE

10 Three dogs—two Pomeranians and a Pekingese—should probably all have been named Lucky. What did these three dogs survive?
a. obedience school
b. the sinking of the *Titanic*
c. a tsunami
d. getting lost at a cat show

11 Reaching speeds up to 45 miles an hour (72 km/h), what breed of dog is the fastest on Earth?
a. Chihuahua
b. Australian shepherd
c. Rhodesian ridgeback
d. greyhound

12 An Australian cattle dog named Bluey is the longest-living dog on record. How long did Bluey live?
a. 3 years and 2 months
b. 19 years and 11 months
c. 29 years and 5 months
d. 45 years

AUSTRALIAN CATTLE DOG

CHECK YOUR ANSWERS ON PAGES 164–165.

White House Pets

1 Which U.S. President had a cat named Socks in the White House?

a. George W. Bush
b. William Jefferson Clinton
c. Harry S. Truman
d. Gerald Ford

2 This U.S. President wrote the Gettysburg Address and owned a pet turkey and two pet goats.

a. George Washington
b. John Quincy Adams
c. Ulysses S. Grant
d. Abraham Lincoln

3 During World War I, which U.S. President raised sheep on the White House lawn and sold their wool to raise money for the American Red Cross?

a. Woodrow Wilson
b. Thomas Jefferson
c. Andrew Jackson
d. Dwight D. Eisenhower

4 Which U.S. President and his family got Macaroni the pony as a gift from Vice President Lyndon B. Johnson?

a. Richard Nixon
b. Franklin Delano Roosevelt
c. John F. Kennedy
d. Barack Obama

5 U.S. President Martin Van Buren got these animals as a gift, but Congress convinced him to give them to the zoo.

a. two tiger cubs
b. a pair of pythons
c. two mules
d. a couple of hippos

6 Teddy bears were named after this U.S. President who kept a lizard, coyote, lion, hyena, zebra, and kangaroo rats at the White House.

a. Jimmy Carter
b. George H. W. Bush
c. Theodore Roosevelt
d. William McKinley

7 U.S. President Calvin Coolidge and his wife built a special house for their "masked" pet, Rebecca. What was Rebecca?

a. a dog
b. a ferret
c. a cat
d. a raccoon

8 This U.S. President had a parrot that actually belonged to his wife, Dolley.

a. James Madison
b. Jimmy Carter
c. Ulysses S. Grant
d. George Washington

9 U.S. President John Quincy Adams kept this unusual pet with large chompers.

a. a walrus
b. an alligator
c. a lion
d. a chicken

10 True or false? Spotty, a springer spaniel, was the only pet to spend time in the White House under two different U.S. Presidents.

11 True or false? U.S. President Benjamin Harrison kept a camel as a pet during his term from 1889 to 1893.

12 The family of U.S. President Barack Obama named their pets Bo and Sunny. What are Bo and Sunny?

a. potbellied pigs
b. Portuguese water dogs
c. goldfish
d. hairless cats

CHECK YOUR ANSWERS ON PAGES 164–165.

Pocket PETS

1 Which of the following rodents are considered to be very social?
a. gerbils
b. rats
c. guinea pigs
d. hamsters

2 What should you do if your hamster's teeth turn yellow?
a. Brush them.
b. Change its diet.
c. Take it to a dentist.
d. Nothing. It's normal.

HAMSTER

3 **True or false?** The smallest gerbil can be as small as about 1.5 inches (3.8 cm) long.

4 Why do you need to give pet rodents wooden chewsticks?
a. to wear down their continually growing teeth
b. because it helps keep them calm
c. so they don't snack too much
d. so they can make the sticks into bedding

5 What is not good to feed a pet mouse?
a. peas
b. apples
c. chocolate
d. food pellets

6 **True or false?** Chinchillas—rodents from South America—can jump several feet in the air.

CHINCHILLA

7 Which rodent is not social and would be content if left alone?

a. guinea pig
b. chinchilla
c. gerbil
d. Sonic the Hedgehog

GUINEA PIG

8 Which was one of the first rodents to be domesticated by humans?

a. hamsters
b. rats
c. squirrels
d. guinea pigs

9 Which is a sign of good fortune at the Karni Mata Temple in India, which was built to honor the Hindu rat goddess?

a. having a rat run across your feet
b. eating food nibbled on by a temple rat
c. spying a rare white rat
d. all of the above

10 Which of the following problems can guinea pigs have if they don't get enough vitamin C?

a. bad breath
b. poor eyesight
c. male-pattern baldness
d. scurvy, a condition that causes bleeding and bone problems

11 Which is a healthful diet choice for small rodents?

a. salt
b. cabbage
c. multivitamins
d. your left shoe

12 **True or false?** There are more than 110 species of gerbils in the world.

GERBIL

CHECK YOUR ANSWERS ON PAGES 164–165.

The X Factor: Pet Edition

1 TWIGGY THE SQUIRREL IS WORLD FAMOUS FOR WATER-SKIING.

2 YOU CAN BUY A PAINTING MADE BY A RACEHORSE FOR $500.

3 KAME-CHAN THE COCKATIEL CAN SING AND DANCE "GANGNAM STYLE."

4 A PERUVIAN SURFER TRAINED HIS PET ALPACA TO SURF WITH HIM.

5 A LOST PARROT IN JAPAN LOCATED ITS OWNER BY REPEATING ITS NAME AND ADDRESS TO THE PEOPLE WHO FOUND IT.

6 TILLMAN THE BULLDOG IS A JUMP-ROPING SENSATION ON YOUTUBE.

7 AMADEUS THE CHIHUAHUA APPEARED ON *THE TONIGHT SHOW* TO SHOWCASE HIS TALENT AS A MARIACHI DANCER.

8 THERE'S A GOLDFISH THAT HAS BEEN TRAINED TO PLAY SOCCER.

9 MUDSLINGER AND DIGGER ARE PET POTBELLIED PIGS WHO CAN PLAY GOLF.

10 A RABBIT IN JAPAN NAMED OOLONG COULD BALANCE MANY KINDS OF OBJECTS ON HIS HEAD.

11 BEARS RAISED BY PEOPLE AND TRAINED TO ACT IN MOVIES ARE TAUGHT HOW TO ROAR AND LOOK EXTRA SCARY.

12 ON THE TV SHOW *BRITAIN'S GOT TALENT*, CHANDI THE RESCUE DOG IMPRESSED THE JUDGES BY DANCING.

13 PANDA, A MINIATURE HORSE, IS A GUIDE FOR HER OWNER, WHO IS BLIND.

14 A CAT IN RUSSIA WORKS AS AN ASSISTANT LIBRARIAN.

15 ONE OF THE WORLD'S SMALLEST HORSES PLAYS WITH A DOG INSTEAD OF WITH OTHER HORSES.

16 THE 13 DOGS IN THE SUPER WAN WAN CIRCUS IN JAPAN HOLD THE WORLD RECORD FOR BREAK DANCING.

17 MISHKA THE HUSKY BECAME AN INTERNET SENSATION BECAUSE SHE MAKES A NOISE THAT MANY PEOPLE THINK SOUNDS LIKE "I LOVE YOU!"

18 FISH CAN BE TAUGHT TO DO TRICKS SUCH AS WEAVING AROUND POLES AND JUMPING THROUGH HOOPS.

19 MUTLEY IS THE ONLY ANIMAL CERTIFIED AS A DEEP-SEA SCUBA DIVING DOG.

20 A RESCUED STRAY CAT NAMED NORA LOVES TO PLAY THE BANJO.

21 A MINIATURE HORSE NAMED NUGGET CAN SPELL WORDS.

22 A PET OPOSSUM NAMED RATATOUILLE LOVES TO SNOWBOARD.

23 JESSIE THE JACK RUSSELL TERRIER CAN MAKE THE BED, MAKE THE COFFEE, MAKE THE TOAST, AND FETCH YOUR TV REMOTE CONTROL.

24 RABBITS CAN BE TRAINED TO USE THE LITTER BOX.

25 EINSTEIN THE PARROT WAS NAMED BECAUSE SHE HAS MESSY WHITE FEATHERS ON TOP OF HER HEAD, MAKING THE BIRD LOOK LIKE FAMOUS SCIENTIST ALBERT EINSTEIN.

26 SWEET PEA IS A RABBIT THAT CAN WALK DOWN STAIRS WHILE BALANCING A GLASS OF WATER.

27 ANASTASIA, A JACK RUSSELL TERRIER, HOLDS THE WORLD RECORD FOR POPPING 100 BALLOONS IN 44.49 SECONDS.

28 IT WAS ONCE TRENDY TO KEEP A PET ROCK.

29 WILLIAM HECKLER TRAINED HIS PET MICE TO JUGGLE.

30 CHAMPIS THE BUNNY LEARNED HOW TO HERD SHEEP FROM WATCHING SOME DOGS DO IT.

CHECK YOUR ANSWERS ON PAGES 164–165.

Aquarium ANTICS

1 What is one way that fiddler crabs are helpful in an aquarium?

FIDDLER CRAB

a. They eat harmful algae.
b. They trim plants with their big claw.
c. They break up fights between other fish.
d. They look tough in there.

2 If a goldfish is given excellent care, how long can it live?

a. up to 1 week
b. 6 months
c. 3 years
d. 20 years or more

3 Which of the following creatures could not live in a freshwater aquarium?

a. minnow
b. rainbow fish
c. horseshoe crab
d. guppy

4 **True or false?** Angelfish are carnivorous, which means they will eat other fish.

ANGELFISH

5 Do catfish help or harm an aquarium environment?

a. Harm. They sneak up on and scare the other fish.
b. Help. They make the other fish look beautiful.
c. Help. They eat up the food other fish don't eat.
d. Harm. They pick fights with the other fish.

FISH IN AN AQUARIUM

6 Sea horses move mainly by doing what?

a. waiting for the ocean current to move them
b. flapping small fins on their backs
c. curling their tails and using them as pogo sticks
d. calling a taxi

7 Which animal is a trendy aquarium pet in Great Britain?

a. piranha
b. stingray
c. jellyfish
d. dogfish

8 **True or false?** A family in Los Angeles, California, U.S.A., has a fish tank the size of a two-car garage.

9 In China, having a pet fish is good luck because the Chinese word for "fish" sounds like which word?

a. wealth
b. water
c. wisdom
d. wish

GUPPY

10 What is one reason guppies are popular in home aquariums?

a. They bear live young.
b. They lay eggs on the sides of the aquarium.
c. They can do tricks.
d. They like to fight with the other fish.

11 What happens when two male Siamese fighting fish see each other?

a. They dance.
b. They attack each other.
c. They give high fives.
d. They make funny faces.

12 Before glass was invented around 50 B.C., ancient Romans kept their pet fish in what?

a. small tanks made of marble
b. small bowls made of clay
c. large ponds carved from stone
d. large tree trunks

SIAMESE FIGHTING FISH

CHECK YOUR ANSWERS ON PAGES 164–165.

Celebrity Pets

1 Fozzi the labradoodle was "born this way." Who is Fozzi's owner?

a. Carrie Underwood
b. Selena Gomez
c. Taylor Swift
d. Lady Gaga

2 Which true-life miracle dolphin starred in *Dolphin Tale*, a movie about the people who saved her life?

a. Flipper
b. Winter
c. Filippo
d. Georgina

3 "I'll get you, my pretty, and your little dog, too!" In which classic movie did a female cairn terrier star?

a. *Home Alone*
b. *The Wizard of Oz*
c. *Homeward Bound*
d. *Twilight*

4 Actor Shia LaBeouf used which social media tool to update his fans about his dog's surgery?

a. Facebook
b. Twitter
c. Instagram
d. live television

5 True or false? The dogs that have portrayed a collie named Lassie have been both males and females.

6 This funny actor's bulldog, Meatball, dressed up in a suit for the actor's wedding.

a. Steve Carell
b. Robert Pattinson
c. Adam Sandler
d. Daniel Radcliffe

7 Which kind of dog does *Twilight* star Kristen Stewart have?

a. a wolf-dog mix
b. a toy poodle
c. a pit bull
d. a bloodhound

8 This popular actress is crazy about sloths. Who is she?

a. Kristen Bell
b. Emma Watson
c. Zendaya
d. Jennifer Lawrence

9 Which celebrity had a pet monkey?

a. Zac Efron
b. Joe Jonas
c. Justin Bieber
d. Channing Tatum

10 What is Katy Perry's cat's name?

a. Kitty Purry
b. Vegas
c. California Gurl
d. Part O'Me

11 In the Harry Potter series, what is the name of Hagrid's three-headed dog?

a. Beastie
b. Growler
c. Fang
d. Fluffy

GAME SHOW

ULTIMATE PET CHALLENGE

1 What is a female cat called?

a. queen
b. mare
c. Catwoman
d. her majesty

2 TRUE OR FALSE? In the 1300s, people thought cats spread the bubonic plague.

3 Why did Europeans bring cats to North America in the 1600s and 1700s?

a. for good luck
b. for bad luck
c. to control mice
d. to scare off wild dogs

4 A medium-size dog that is ten years old is about the same age as someone who is how old?

a. 5 years old
b. 10 years old
c. 60 years old
d. 100 years old

5 A sugar glider is a pet most closely related to which animal?

a. bear
b. squirrel
c. cat
d. horse

6 Why should you not shout "Boo!" at pet rabbits?

a. They may bite if startled.
b. They cry easily.
c. Their ears are sensitive.
d. Their moms wouldn't like it.

7 Which is the number one health issue among dogs?

a. cat bites
b. obesity
c. fur balls
d. chocolate poisoning

BEAGLE

ENGLISH BULLDOG

8 **TRUE OR FALSE?** A cat trekked alone more than 1,300 miles (2,092 km) through Siberia to be with its family.

9 What pets communicate by whinnying, nickering, squealing, and grunting?
a. horses
b. cats
c. guinea pigs
d. younger brothers and sisters

GUINEA PIG

10 What kind of animal was Charlotte, best friend to Wilbur the pig in *Charlotte's Web*?
a. mouse
b. cat
c. cow
d. spider

12 The blue hyacinth macaw is from Brazil. It is the largest bird in the macaw family. How wide is its wingspan?
a. about the length of a school bus
b. about the length of two skateboards
c. about the length of a notebook
d. about the length of a surfboard

11 In which movie will you find the characters Pongo and Perdita, the pets of Roger and Anita Radcliffe?
a. *Cinderella*
b. *Lady and the Tramp*
c. *101 Dalmatians*
d. *Snow White*

13 **TRUE OR FALSE?** Lulu, a potbellied pig, saved a heart-attack victim by running out of the house and lying down in traffic until someone stopped to help.

14 In the 1870s, this animal was the first of its kind to enter the United States, and it became a White House pet.

a. Siamese fighting fish
b. Siamese cat
c. armadillo
d. macaw parrot

15 **ULTIMATE BRAIN BUSTER**
WHAT BREED OF DOG IS SCOOBY-DOO?

CHECK YOUR ANSWERS ON PAGES 164–165.

Big Ideas

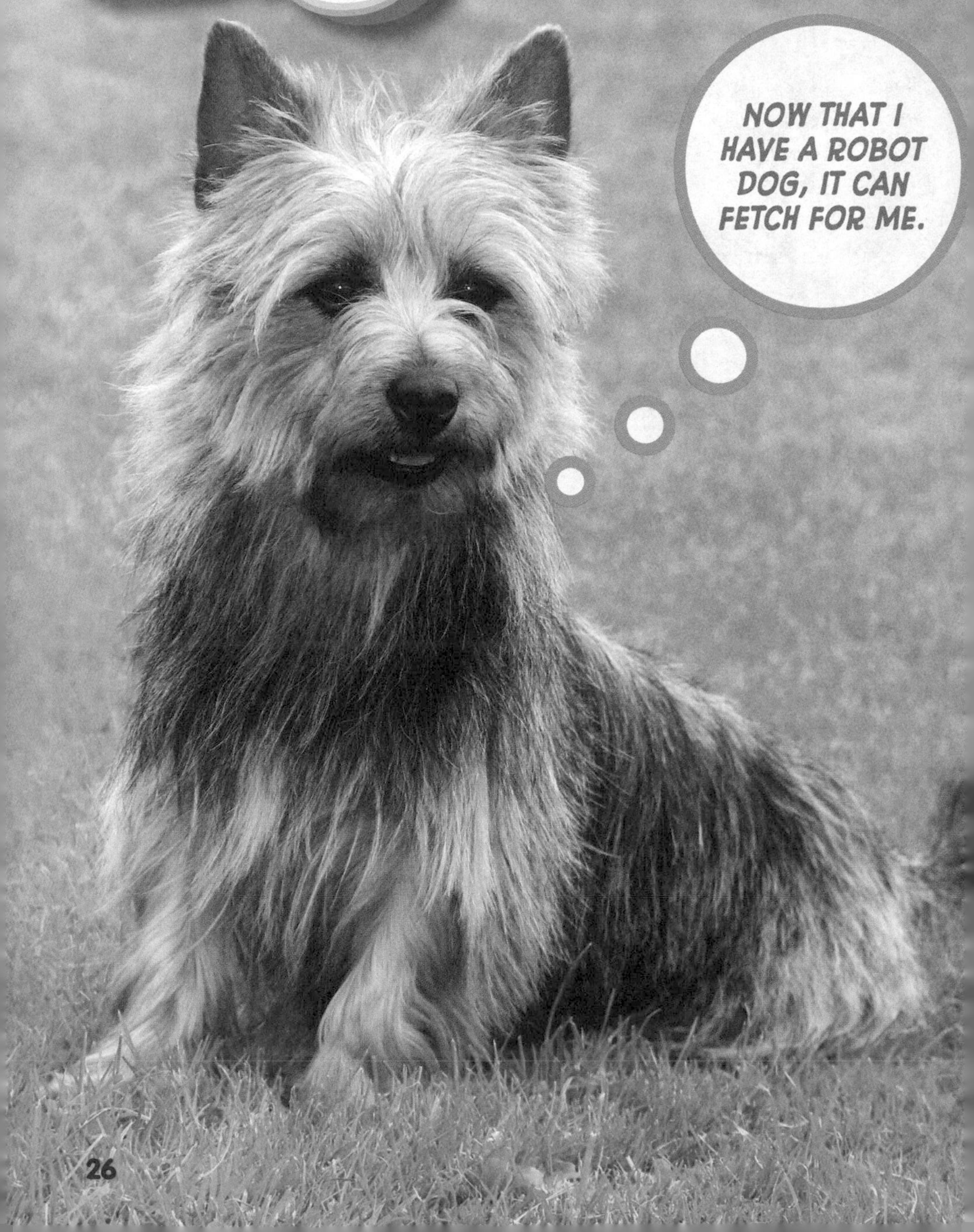

Water WONDERS

1. **True or false?** Scientists have made fake teeth for sharks that have lost their teeth.

2. **Daredevil surfers have used Jet Skis to surf waves made by _____.**
   a. tsunamis
   b. glaciers
   c. submarines
   d. pods of whales

3. **In 1901, Annie Taylor was the first person to survive going over Niagara Falls in a _____.**
   a. rowboat
   b. diving suit
   c. barrel
   d. Jet Ski

4. **Which of these was the first craft to travel across a large body of water?**

   a. steamship

   b. sailboat

   c. ferry

   d. dugout canoe

5. **Which inventive founder of the United States of America created swim fins for hands?**
   a. Benjamin Franklin
   b. John Adams
   c. George Washington
   d. John Hancock

6. **True or false?** In 2013, the Mars rover Opportunity discovered a large river with flowing water on Mars.

MARS ROVER

Big Ideas

JACQUES COUSTEAU

7 *Hydroptere* is a sailboat that can _____.
a. recycle water
b. fly above the water
c. dive underwater
d. drop its sails into the water

8 Émile Gagnan and Jacques Cousteau made the first workable diving gear in 1943. What was it called?
a. Aqua Lung
b. EmJaquet
c. Diver Duds
d. Scuba-Do

9 Riding in a bare-bones, human-powered submarine, pilots must wear _____.
a. snorkels
b. name badges
c. scuba gear
d. swim suits

10 Scientists study the undersea environment and live in an underwater laboratory off the coast of _____.
a. Oklahoma, U.S.A.
b. California, U.S.A.
c. Michigan, U.S.A.
d. Florida, U.S.A.

11 What powered early clocks in China?
a. water
b. horses
c. coal
d. magic

CHECK YOUR ANSWERS ON PAGES 165–166.

Out of This World

1 What is working outside of a spacecraft called?

a. space work
b. play time
c. extravehicular activity
d. recess

2 The visor that protects astronauts from the sun's rays is coated with a layer of _____.

a. Kryptonite
b. gold
c. titanium
d. tinfoil

3 What device worn like a backpack helps astronauts move around in space?

a. fiberglass wings
b. rotating propellers
c. birthday balloons
d. nitrogen-jet thrusters

4 Astronauts wear a communications cap under their helmets. It's black and white and is named for the cartoon character _____.

a. Snoopy
c. Garfield
b. Mickey Mouse
d. Scooby-Doo

5 Why do astronauts wear long underwear that contains 300 feet (91.5 m) of water-filled tubes?

a. for a quick drink
b. in case the ship springs a leak
c. to prevent dry skin
d. to keep them cool

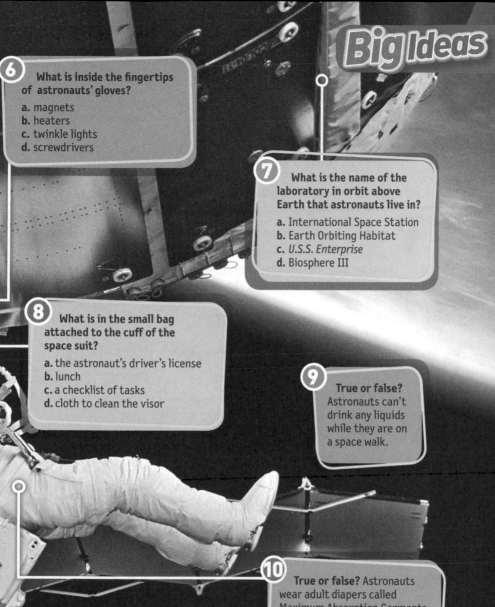

6 What is inside the fingertips of astronauts' gloves?

a. magnets
b. heaters
c. twinkle lights
d. screwdrivers

7 What is the name of the laboratory in orbit above Earth that astronauts live in?

a. International Space Station
b. Earth Orbiting Habitat
c. *U.S.S. Enterprise*
d. Biosphere III

8 What is in the small bag attached to the cuff of the space suit?

a. the astronaut's driver's license
b. lunch
c. a checklist of tasks
d. cloth to clean the visor

9 True or false? Astronauts can't drink any liquids while they are on a space walk.

10 True or false? Astronauts wear adult diapers called Maximum Absorption Garments (MAGs).

AN ASTRONAUT WORKING OUTSIDE OF A SPACECRAFT

11 Which of these is the name of a tool that astronauts use?

a. phaser
b. lightsaber
c. sonic screwdriver
d. pistol-grip hand drill

Gizmos, Gadgets, and Gear

1 U.S. PRESIDENT JOHN F. KENNEDY SAID THAT THE INTERNET HELPED HIM WIN THE ELECTION IN 1960.

2 THE FIRST LIGHTBULBS LASTED FOR JUST ONE HOUR.

3 THE ROOMBA IS A ROBOTIC VACUUM CLEANER.

4 ALTHOUGH IT WAS NEVER MADE, ONE INVENTOR DESIGNED A DEVICE TO SEND GIANT SNOWBALLS FROM ANTARCTICA TO THE DESERT.

5 THE FASTEST A PERSON HAS SOLVED A RUBIK'S CUBE USING ONLY HIS OR HER FEET IS 27.93 SECONDS.

6 DUCT TAPE WAS ORIGINALLY CALLED "DUCK TAPE."

7 THE FIRST LUNCHBOX MADE JUST FOR KIDS HAD A PICTURE OF A COWBOY AND HIS HORSE ON IT.

8 AN EARLY STAPLER MADE FOR KING LOUIS XV OF FRANCE USED GOLD STAPLES.

9 A UNIVERSAL TRANSLATOR, LIKE THE ONE THAT *STAR TREK* CHARACTERS USE TO TALK TO THOSE SPEAKING ANOTHER LANGUAGE, IS NOW REAL.

10 THE COMPUTER MOUSE GOT ITS NAME BECAUSE IT HAD A TAIL AT ONE END.

11 AN EARLY VERSION OF TOOTHPASTE HAD SOAP IN IT.

12 THE SWISS ARMY KNIFE WAS FIRST MADE FOR THE POLISH ARMY.

13 MORE THAN FIVE BILLION PEOPLE USE MOBILE PHONES WORLDWIDE.

14 THE MICKEY MOUSE WATCH WAS INTRODUCED IN 1993.

15 AN EARLY NAME FOR MATCHES WAS "FIRE INCH STICKS."

16 EARLY TV REMOTE CONTROLS HURT DOGS' EARS.

17 THE SUPER SOAKER WATER GUN WAS INVENTED BY AN OLYMPIC SWIMMING CHAMPION.

18 THE HANDHELD TALKING SPELLING BEE SAYS A WORD AND YOU SPELL IT ON THE KEYBOARD.

19 SUNGLASSES WERE FIRST SOLD IN HOLLYWOOD, CALIFORNIA, U.S.A.

20 THE GAME OF LEAF BLOWER HOCKEY WAS INVENTED IN MASSACHUSETTS, U.S.A.

21 ZIPPERS WERE AROUND IN THE 1920s.

22 THE KINDLE WAS THE FIRST E-READER.

23 THE FLASHLIGHT GOT ITS NAME BECAUSE SOLDIERS USED IT TO FLASH SIGNALS TO EACH OTHER.

24 THE SONY WALKMAN WAS SO POPULAR THAT THE WORD "WALKMAN" IS NOW IN THE DICTIONARY.

25 THE SPORK, A COMBINATION SPOON AND FORK, WAS THE EARLIEST KNOWN EATING UTENSIL.

26 THE FIRST WRISTWATCH WAS MADE FOR PEOPLE WHO WERE FISHING SO THEY COULD CHECK THE TIME WITHOUT LETTING GO OF THEIR REELS.

27 IN 1909, A SCIENTIST PREDICTED THE INVENTION OF TEXT MESSAGING.

28 FIGHTER PILOTS IN WORLD WAR II WERE AMONG THE FIRST TO USE BALLPOINT PENS.

29 THE IPOD GOT ITS NAME FROM THE MOVIE *2001: A SPACE ODYSSEY*.

30 ONLY 500,000 GAMEBOY SYSTEMS HAVE SOLD SINCE THE FIRST ONE IN 1989.

CHECK YOUR ANSWERS ON PAGES 165-166.

On the MOVE

1 What early wooden vehicle with metal tires was nicknamed the "bone shaker"?
- a. skateboard
- b. bicycle
- c. wooden car
- d. roller coaster

2 **True or false?** In 2011, fewer than 50 superfast Bugatti Veyron Super Sport automobiles were built.

3 Which of the following have improved athletes' speed and overall performance?
- a. team uniforms
- b. sports drinks
- c. referee whistles
- d. athletic shoes

4 The fastest elevator in the world is in the Taipei 101 building. How long does it take the elevator to climb all 89 stories?
- a. 2 seconds
- b. 15 seconds
- c. 39 seconds
- d. 501 seconds

TAIPEI 101 BUILDING

5 In the 18th century, which army trained and traveled on skis?
- a. Swedish
- b. American
- c. Australian
- d. French

6 The Shinkansen in Japan is one of the world's fastest trains. About how fast does it travel?
- a. 60 miles an hour (96 km/h)
- b. 198 miles an hour (320 km/h)
- c. 403 miles an hour (650 km/h)
- d. 1,234 miles an hour (1,985 km/h)

STEALTH F117A

7 How did the stealth fighter F117A Nighthawk avoid detection?

a. It looked like the enemy's own aircraft.
b. It was coated in a special material that hid it from radar.
c. It put on Harry Potter's Cloak of Invisibility.
d. It moved too quickly for detection.

8 **True or false?** The first waffle soles for running shoes were made by pouring rubber into a waffle iron.

9 The *Gossamer Albatross* set a flight record when it became the first human-powered plane to cross _____.

a. a highway
b. the English Channel
c. Antarctica
d. the Forbidden Forest

GOSSAMER ALBATROSS

10 **True or false?** Soldiers use devices similar to a vacuum cleaner to help them stick to any walls they must climb.

FORMULA ROSSA

11 What are riders on the superfast Formula Rossa roller coaster required to wear?

a. helmets
b. novelty T-shirts
c. bow ties
d. goggles

Ideas for Tomorrow

1 Scientists in California, U.S.A., are working on a _____ that makes DNA. One day it will help them grow new organs for humans.

a. plant
b. vitamin
c. laser printer
d. microwave oven

2 Diners of the future might one day be able to track their calories using a device that _____ their plates.

a. scans
b. weighs
c. smells
d. cleans

3 How are drones used to help sick people?

a. to carry organ transplants
b. to bring medicine to hard-to-reach places
c. to locate outbreaks of disease
d. to find doctors

4 An inventor won an award for creating an inexpensive cardboard bike. About how much did he think it would cost to build each bike?

a. $100.00
b. $30.00
c. $12.00
d. $1.00

5 A new type of alarm clock will not shut off until you _____.

a. answer questions correctly
b. sing a song
c. do ten jumping jacks
d. stare at the clock's face with your eyes open

6 This three-wheel vehicle is both a car and an airplane. What is its name?

a. Batmobile
b. Magic School Bus
c. Millennium Falcon
d. Switchblade

7 How long was the longest human-powered flight?

a. 50 seconds
b. 6 minutes
c. 30 minutes
d. 1 hour

REMOTE-CONTROLLED DRONE

8 NASA is working on a new kind of 3-D printer. What will it print for astronauts going on long missions?

a. food
b. oxygen tanks
c. cell phones
d. space suits

10 Which of these is an invention that may soon take off with people wanting to travel far without a car?

a. a bicycle with a rocket attached
b. a personal aircraft with a propeller in the back
c. a helicopter hat you strap to your head
d. shoes that let you jump hundreds of feet in the air

9 True or false? Scientists now "beam people up" like they did in *Star Trek*.

11 Which feature might bicycle helmets have in the future to make riding safer?

a. a megaphone
b. GPS
c. turn signals
d. a sports drink holder

12 True or false? A company is designing personal jet packs for people to get to work in busy cities.

CHECK YOUR ANSWERS ON PAGES 165-166.

Smart ANIMALS

1 How do gorillas use branches?

a. as walking sticks
b. to test water depth
c. to build bridges
d. all of the above

GORILLA

2 **True or false?** Crows have been seen dropping nuts onto busy streets and retrieving the insides after cars have cracked the shells.

OCTOPUS

3 How might an octopus use a coconut shell?

a. as a bowl
b. to wear as armor
c. to play as a drum
d. to listen to as a radio

4 How do dolphins use large spiral shells called conch shells?

a. to catch small fish
b. to hear the ocean
c. to call for help
d. to give as gifts

5 **True or false?** Orangutans use rolled-up leaves as whistles to warn other orangutans of enemies.

6 Sea otters use stones or shells to _____.

a. open shellfish
b. make music
c. play catch
d. scare off predators

DIGGER WASP

7 **True or false?** Female digger wasps leave a path of stones to show their larvae where to find food.

8 How do elephants use palm fronds or sticks?
a. as fly swatters
b. as tick removers
c. as back scratchers
d. all of the above

9 What creature sometimes uses scrap paper as a sponge for bathing?
a. a clownfish
b. a raven
c. SpongeBob SquarePants
d. a chipmunk

CLOWNFISH

10 What does a woodpecker finch use to get insects out of its burrow?
a. a plastic knife
b. a pebble
c. a song
d. a cactus spine

11 Why would a dresser crab carry a sea anemone on its back?
a. to keep warm
b. to look fancy
c. to hide from its enemies
d. to make the anemone say, "Whee!"

DRESSER CRAB

CHECK YOUR ANSWERS ON PAGES 165-166.

MAP MANIA!
You Saw It Here First

1 KITES
Kites were first used over 3,000 years ago in this large country.

2 RETURNING BOOMERANGS
Returning boomerangs were used to hunt for food while in "the bush."

3 ELECTRIC GUITARS
Electric guitars were first used to play country and jazz music here.

4 BREATH MINTS
Breath mints were invented here so people wouldn't have "mummy breath."

5 PIZZA
Pizza has been eaten here for more than 200 years.

U.S.

NORTH AMERICA

UNITED STATES

UNITED KINGDOM

ATLANTIC OCEAN

PACIFIC OCEAN

SOUTH AMERICA

ANTARCTICA

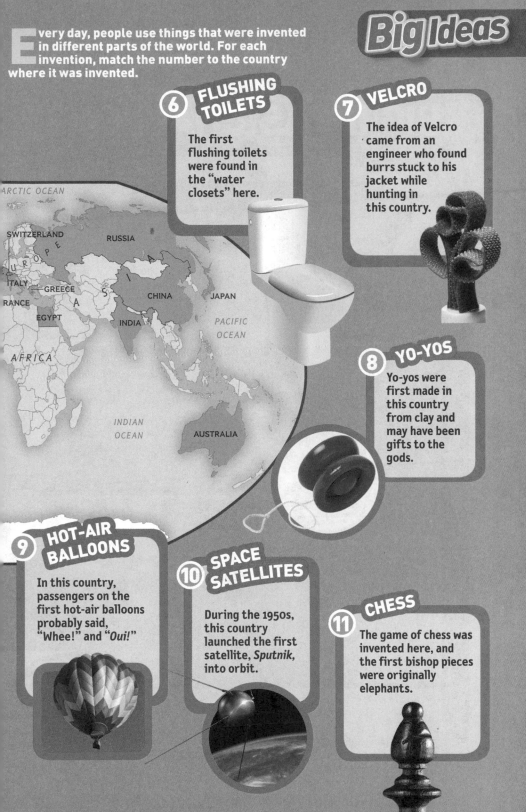

Every day, people use things that were invented in different parts of the world. For each invention, match the number to the country where it was invented.

Big Ideas

6 FLUSHING TOILETS

The first flushing toilets were found in the "water closets" here.

7 VELCRO

The idea of Velcro came from an engineer who found burrs stuck to his jacket while hunting in this country.

8 YO-YOS

Yo-yos were first made in this country from clay and may have been gifts to the gods.

9 HOT-AIR BALLOONS

In this country, passengers on the first hot-air balloons probably said, "Whee!" and *"Oui!"*

10 SPACE SATELLITES

During the 1950s, this country launched the first satellite, *Sputnik*, into orbit.

11 CHESS

The game of chess was invented here, and the first bishop pieces were originally elephants.

ARCTIC OCEAN

SWITZERLAND
RUSSIA
EUROPE
ITALY
GREECE
FRANCE
ASIA
CHINA
JAPAN
EGYPT
INDIA
PACIFIC OCEAN
AFRICA
INDIAN OCEAN
AUSTRALIA

GAME SHOW

ULTIMATE BIG IDEAS CHALLENGE

1 Where did Wilbur and Orville Wright build their first flying airplane?
a. Paris, France
b. Boston, Massachusetts
c. Kitty Hawk, North Carolina
d. Tokyo, Japan

2 The oldest known surfboard was 148 pounds (67 kg) and made of solid _____.
a. steel
b. plastic
c. whale bones
d. wood

3 The Gate Tower Building in crowded Osaka, Japan, is special because _____.
a. a highway runs through it
b. it is partially underwater
c. it holds more than one million people
d. it is also a giant robot

4 The first astronaut to travel to space came from which country?
a. U.S.A.
b. the Soviet Union (Russia)
c. China
d. Rocketonia

5 Doctors in China helped a man with a deformed nose by doing what?
a. growing a new nose on the man's forehead
b. giving him a robotic nose
c. giving him glasses and a fake nose
d. cutting his nose off entirely

6 TRUE OR FALSE?
Nobody has ever traveled around the world in a hot-air balloon.

7 TRUE OR FALSE?
Inventors are working on a fork that measures how fast you eat your food.

42

8 Long before iPhones and Instagram, there was this first portable camera with a delicious name.

a. Kodak Brownie
b. Polaroid Cupcake
c. Apple aPhone
d. Picture McNugget

9 All of these were developed from NASA technology except _____.

a. a thermometer that can be swallowed
b. cordless tools
c. memory foam mattresses
d. scratch-resistant sun-glass lenses

10 Which of the following was invented in Spain?

a. acoustic guitar
b. battery
c. parachute
d. toilet paper

11 TRUE OR FALSE?

Mother bottlenose dolphins teach their young to use sponges as tools.

12 Which of the following countries does not have a high-speed train?

a. Germany
b. China
c. Italy
d. Brazil

13 In which country was the first video game invented?

a. Japan
b. U.S.A.
c. China
d. Australia

14 Which of these is said to be the most powerful communication tool ever invented?

a. World Wide Web
b. telephone
c. telegraph
d. pencil

15 ULTIMATE BRAIN BUSTER

WHICH VEHICLE WAS FIRST SUCCESSFULLY DESIGNED IN THE SOVIET UNION (RUSSIA) BUT DEVELOPED IN THE U.S.A. WHEN THE INVENTOR MOVED?

a. moped
b. Segway
c. Jet Ski
d. helicopter

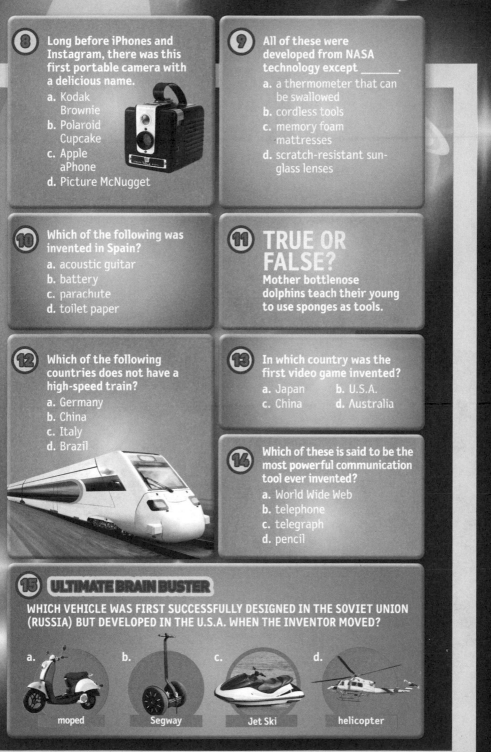

Pop Culture

DID YOU KNOW?
THE DIARY OF A WIMPY KID SERIES INCLUDES EIGHT BOOKS, THREE MOVIES, AND MORE. THIS SCENE IS FROM THE 2011 FILM DIARY OF A WIMPY KID: RODRICK RULES.

Toy Stories

1 Which putty-like material was invented in the 1950s to clean wallpaper but today is used by kids in arts-and-crafts projects?
a. paste
b. pancake batter
c. Play-Doh
d. WALL-E

2 **True or False?** HexBugs are micro, robotic, insectlike toys that react to their environment.

BARBIE DOLL

HEXBUG

3 Barbie fashion dolls have portrayed all the following careers except _____.
a. fighter pilot
b. architect
c. farmer
d. President

SLINKY

4 What did a Slinky toy do when scientists aboard the space shuttle *Discovery* played with it?
a. It unwound.
b. It did not float.
c. It walked up stairs.
d. It did not slink at all.

5 Which company created the Xbox?
a. Apple
b. Boxes-R-Us
c. Microsoft
d. Xerox

FURBY

6 An online dictionary and app can help you communicate with an interactive Furby toy. What language does Furby speak?
a. Furbese
b. Furbalian
c. Fur Latin
d. Furbish

7 Which of the following is not a name of a Monster High fashion doll?

a. Ghoulia Yelps
b. Cruela D'Zilla
c. Clawdeen Wolf
d. Draculaura

8 How many kids can fit comfortably in the largest Radio Flyer wagon ever built?

a. 7
b. 15
c. 1,000
d. 75

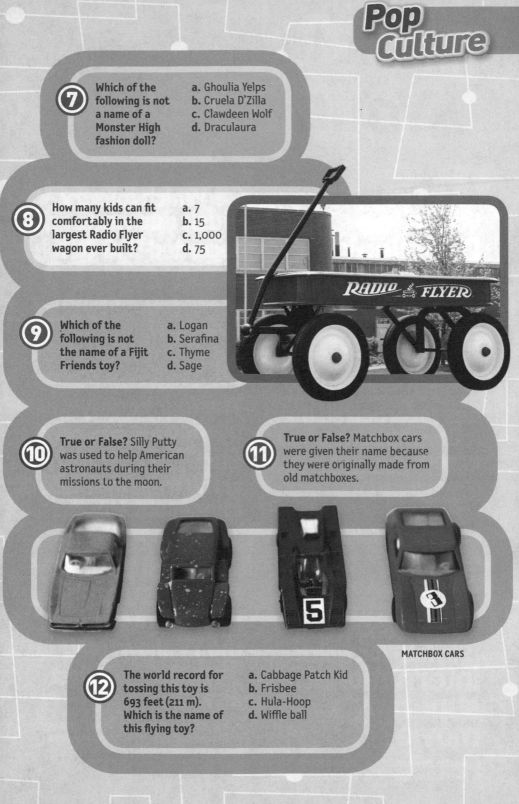

RADIO FLYER

9 Which of the following is not the name of a Fijit Friends toy?

a. Logan
b. Serafina
c. Thyme
d. Sage

10 True or False? Silly Putty was used to help American astronauts during their missions to the moon.

11 True or False? Matchbox cars were given their name because they were originally made from old matchboxes.

MATCHBOX CARS

12 The world record for tossing this toy is 693 feet (211 m). Which is the name of this flying toy?

a. Cabbage Patch Kid
b. Frisbee
c. Hula-Hoop
d. Wiffle ball

CHECK YOUR ANSWERS ON PAGES 167–168.

Music to Your Ears

1 Which was the title of **One Direction's** first official song?

a. "I Want It That Way"
b. "What Makes You Beautiful"
c. "Loved You First"
d. "Who Makes Your Dinner"

2 Which country music duo wrote and recorded **the hit song "Cruise"?**

a. Florida Offensive Line
b. Brooks & Dunn
c. Sugarland
d. Florida Georgia Line

3 **Taylor Swift** has recorded all the following songs except _____.

a. "We Are Never Ever Getting Back Together"
b. "Our Song"
c. "Beautiful Ears"
d. "I Knew You Were Trouble"

4 **True or False?** The four hockey-playing members of **Big Time Rush** come from the state of Minnesota, U.S.A.

5 **Adele** won an Academy Award for her song "Skyfall" for which **international superspy's movie?**

a. Austin Powers
b. James Bond
c. Harriet the Spy
d. Agent Cody Banks

6 Which **country music superstar** has been a coach on the TV show *The Voice* since it first aired?

a. Miranda Lambert
b. Kenny Chesney
c. Blake Shelton
d. Sandy Cheeks

7 Which reality singing competition did singer **Carrie Underwood** win?

a. *The X Factor*
b. *The Biggest Loser*
c. *The Voice*
d. *American Idol*

8 True or False? Josh Groban is the lead singer for the band **Maroon 5.**

9 Which is the title of Canadian singer **Carly Rae Jepsen's** song that has been downloaded more than 12 million times?

a. "Love Story"
b. "Call Me Maybe"
c. "Call Me Al"
d. "Tiny Little Bows"

10 By which name are some of **Justin Bieber's** biggest fans known?

a. the Biebs
b. Bieberites
c. Big Biebers
d. Beliebers

11 Which music star provided the voice for the character Artie in the movie *Shrek the Third*?

a. Justin Timberlake
b. Will Smith
c. Bruno Mars
d. Adam Levine

12 Who recorded "Love You Like a Love Song" and appeared on the TV show *Wizards of Waverly Place*?

a. Selena Gomez
b. Mila Kunis
c. Shakira
d. Emma Roberts

The Book Club

SCOTT O'DELL
Island of the Blue Dolphins

(1) Who moves into the Heffley house and causes aggravation in *Diary of a Wimpy Kid: The Third Wheel*?

a. Benjy
b. Rowley Jefferson
c. Uncle Gary
d. Aunt Loretta

(2) In the novel *Charlotte's Web*, what kind of animal is Templeton?

a. a dog
b. a spider
c. a pig
d. a rat

(3) Karana, the main character in *Island of the Blue Dolphins*, is also known as Won-a-pa-lei, which means _____.

a. "Girl Who Lives Alone"
b. "Girl With Long Black Hair"
c. "Daughter of the Chief"
d. "Girl Who Swims With Dolphins"

(4) What does Dumbledore leave to Harry in his will in *Harry Potter and the Deathly Hallows*?

a. the Deluminator
b. the Invisibility Cloak
c. a Golden Snitch
d. the book *The Tales of Beedle and Bard*

(5) True or False? *The Hunger Games* takes place in a nation called District 12.

DUMBLEDORE

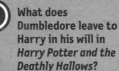

JASPER FFORDE
THE *Last Dragonslayer*

THE CHRONICLES OF KAZAM: BOOK ONE

(6) Who is the narrator of the book *The Last Dragonslayer*?

a. Jasper Fforde
b. King Snodd IV
c. Doug the Dragon
d. Quarkbeast

(7) In the novel *Where the Red Fern Grows*, Billy saves his money for two years to buy what?

a. two redbone coonhound puppies
b. two red fern plants
c. two baby raccoons
d. two red shoes

STANLEY YELNATS AND HECTOR ZERONI IN *HOLES*

(8) **True or False?** In the *A Series of Unfortunate Events* book series, Lemony Snicket is a private detective.

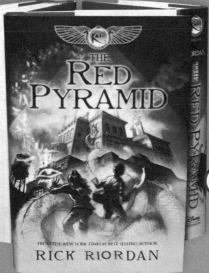

(9) In the novel *Holes*, why is Stanley Yelnats forced to dig holes every day?

a. to search for water
b. to look for a lost treasure
c. to build his muscles
d. for the fun of it

(10) **True or False?** In the *Kane Chronicles* novels, Apophis is a chaos snake.

(11) Which special ability do Mrs. Whatsit, Mrs. Who, and Mrs. Which have in the novel *A Wrinkle in Time*?

a. They can travel across long stretches of time and space.
b. They can remove the worst stains from any surface.
c. They can solve incredibly difficult math problems.
d. They can sing the words to every song ever written.

THE RED PYRAMID

FROM THE NEW YORK TIMES #1 BEST-SELLING AUTHOR

RICK RIORDAN

Disney HYPERION

(12) What is Farley Drexel Hatcher's nickname in the book *Tales of a Fourth Grade Nothing*?

a. Fudge
b. Pudding
c. Brat
d. Hatch

Tons of Toons

1 THE ORIGINAL *TOM AND JERRY* CARTOON SERIES WON SEVEN ACADEMY AWARDS.

2 THE BOOK OF RULES THAT COSMO AND WANDA FOLLOW IN THE TV SHOW *THE FAIRLY ODDPARENTS* IS CALLED *RULES FOR FAIRY DUMMIES*.

3 IN THE TV SHOW *SPONGEBOB SQUAREPANTS*, THE CHARACTER PLANKTON'S REAL NAME IS HERSCHEL.

4 OCHO IS AN EIGHT-BIT SPIDER WHO SPEAKS IN BEEPS AND BLIPS IN THE TV SHOW *THE AMAZING WORLD OF GUMBALL*.

5 IN THE HOLIDAY CLASSIC CARTOON SPECIAL *FROSTY THE SNOWMAN*, A MAGIC BROOM BRINGS FROSTY TO LIFE.

6 O.W.C.A., IN THE *PHINEAS AND FERB* TV SHOW, STANDS FOR "ORGANIZATION WITHOUT A COOL ACRONYM."

7 IN *THE PENGUINS OF MADAGASCAR* TELEVISION SHOW, KING JULIEN IS AN OTTER.

8 *MONSTERS, INC.* WAS THE FIRST FEATURE-LENGTH COMPUTER-ANIMATED MOVIE.

9 THE MAIN CHARACTERS IN THE ANIMATED SERIES *FULLMETAL ALCHEMIST* ARE TWIN GIRLS.

10 ETHAN AND PEACHES IN THE MOVIE *ICE AGE: CONTINENTAL DRIFT* ARE BROTHER AND SISTER.

11 MORDECAI AND RIGBY WORK AS WAITERS IN A COFFEE SHOP ON THE *REGULAR SHOW* TV SHOW.

12 THE BOSS OF THE ANTI-VILLAIN LEAGUE IS SILAS RAMSBOTTOM IN THE MOVIE *DESPICABLE ME 2*.

13 BUGS BUNNY'S HOMETOWN IS BROOKLYN, NEW YORK, U.S.A.

14 FRED FLINTSTONE, FROM THE CLASSIC TV SHOW *THE FLINTSTONES*, IS NICKNAMED "TWINKLETOES" BECAUSE OF HIS AMAZING DANCE MOVES.

15 IN THE CLASSIC CARTOON SERIES *THE JETSONS*, GEORGE AND HIS FAMILY HAVE A PET CAT NAMED ASTRO.

16 IN THE CLASSIC *SCOOBY-DOO* CARTOON SERIES, SCABBY-DOO IS THE NAME OF SCOOBY'S LITTLE NEPHEW.

17 GARFIELD'S FAVORITE FOOD IS LASAGNA IN THE *GARFIELD* COMIC STRIP.

18 RUSSELL IS A MEMBER OF THE URBAN EXPLORERS IN THE MOVIE *UP*.

19 IN THE TV SHOW *DEXTER'S LABORATORY*, DEXTER'S MOM HELPS HIM WITH HIS EXPERIMENTS.

20 LUCY IS CHARLIE BROWN'S SISTER IN THE *PEANUTS* COMIC STRIP.

21 BUZZ AND DELETE ARE THE NAMES OF HACKER'S HENCHMEN ON THE TV SHOW *CYBERCHASE*.

22 "I YAM WHAT I YAM" IS AN EXPRESSION MADE FAMOUS BY THE CLASSIC CARTOON CHARACTER PORKY PIG.

23 LUIGI, THE TIRE-CHANGING OWNER OF LUIGI'S CASA DELLA TIRES IN THE MOVIE *CARS 2*, IS FOND OF MERCEDES-BENZ AUTOMOBILES.

24 NEIL PATRICK HARRIS PROVIDES THE VOICE FOR GRU, THE MAIN CHARACTER IN THE *DESPICABLE ME* MOVIES.

25 IN THE TV SHOW *AVATAR: THE LAST AIRBENDER*, SOKKA IS THE NAME OF THE LAST AIRBENDER.

26 BULLWINKLE THE MOOSE, FROM THE CLASSIC CARTOON SERIES *THE ROCKY AND BULLWINKLE SHOW*, WENT TO COLLEGE AT WOSSAMOTTA U.

27 GINORMICA, FROM THE MOVIE *MONSTERS VS. ALIENS*, WAS BITTEN BY A SPIDER ON HER WEDDING DAY, WHICH CHANGED HER DNA.

28 THE ICE KING IN THE CARTOON NETWORK TV SHOW *ADVENTURE TIME* WAS ONCE KNOWN AS SIMON PETRIKOV, A STUDENT OF ANCIENT ARTIFACTS.

29 DAFFY DUCK OFTEN ENDS CLASSIC *LOONEY TUNES* TV SHOWS BY SAYING, "THAT'S ALL, FOLKS!"

30 IN THE CLASSIC TV SERIES *THE ROAD RUNNER SHOW*, WILE E. COYOTE OFTEN USES PRODUCTS FROM THE ACME COMPANY TO TRY TO CAPTURE THE ROAD RUNNER.

Famous PAIRS

ROBIN AND BATMAN

1 At whose home do Woody and Buzz end up at the end of the movie *Toy Story 3*?
a. Andy's
b. Sid's
c. Bonnie's
d. Lotso's

2 When not wearing their crime-fighting capes, Batman and Robin are known as _____ and _____.
a. Peter Parker and Dexter Bennett
b. Bruce Banner and Jim Wilson
c. Bruce Wayne and Dick Grayson
d. Clark Kent and Jimmy Olsen

3 Who travels with and protects his fellow Hobbit, Frodo Baggins, during many adventures in *The Lord of the Rings* movies?
a. Bilbo Baggins
b. Grima Wormtongue
c. Dandumb Smith
d. Samwise Gamgee

FRODO

4 Which TV best friends dined on spaghetti tacos?
a. Bert and Ernie
b. Carly and Sam
c. Flick and Flack
d. Drake and Josh

5 **True or False?** *Animaniacs* television show characters Pinky and the Brain are mice.

6 Which pop culture legends fell in love on the set of their first television commercial for Mattel Toys in 1961?
a. Fred and Wilma Flintstone
b. Mr. and Mrs. Potato Head
c. Barbie and Ken
d. Daffy Duck and Daisy Duck

WILMA AND FRED FLINTSTONE

54

Pop Culture

7 What are the names of the two friends who use science to prove or disprove popular myths on the TV show *MythBusters*?

a. Simon and Randy
b. Calvin and Hobbes
c. Thelma and Daphne
d. Jamie and Adam

8 **True or False?** Mario and Luigi from the Mario Bros. video games are two New York City cousins who are musicians.

9 In the *Legend of Zelda* games, Link must often rescue Princess Zelda in which fictional setting?

a. Hyrule
b. Narnia
c. Oz
d. No-rules

10 Who is one of Brick Heck's best friends on the TV show *The Middle*?

a. Brad
b. Carly
c. his backpack
d. his no. 2 pencil

MARIO AND LUIGI

11 In which decade did Mickey and Minnie Mouse share their first kiss?

a. the 1920s
b. the 1950s
c. the 1960s
d. the 1980s

12 Which school of study do movie monster friends Mike and Sulley attend at Monsters University?

a. School of Scaring
b. School of Liberal Arts & Monstrosities
c. School of Business
d. School of Engineering

MIKE AND SULLEY
FROM *MONSTERS, INC.*

CHECK YOUR ANSWERS ON PAGES 167–168.

Heroes and Heroines

1 THE FIRST BATMAN MOVIE WAS MADE IN 1966.

2 IN THE POPULAR CARTOON SERIES *SCOOBY-DOO*, SHAGGY SHAKES ARE USED TO MOTIVATE SHAGGY AND SCOOBY TO PARTICIPATE IN DANGEROUS CRIME-SOLVING CAPERS.

3 GREEN LANTERN'S POWER RING IS FUELED BY LOVE.

4 STORM, FROM THE X-MEN COMIC BOOK SERIES, WAS THE FIRST AFRICAN AMERICAN FEMALE COMIC BOOK CHARACTER WITH A SUPPORTING ROLE IN MARVEL COMICS AND DC COMICS.

5 PRINCESS MERIDA IN THE MOVIE *BRAVE* USES A BOW AND ARROW.

6 IN THE *LORD OF THE RINGS* FILM SERIES, ARAGORN'S SWORD IS NAMED HERUGRIM.

7 IN THE FILM *STAR WARS*, HAN SOLO PILOTED A STAR SHIP CALLED THE *MILLENNIUM FALCON*.

8 SUPERMAN HAS A SUPERDOG NAMED KRYPTO.

9 IN *ICE AGE: CONTINENTAL DRIFT*, MANNY DESCRIBES HIS HOMETOWN AS "TWELVE DAYS NORTH OF HOPELESS AND A FEW DEGREES SOUTH OF FREEZING TO DEATH."

10 IN THE *HARRY POTTER* FILM AND BOOK SERIES, HERMIONE GRANGER'S PATRONUS TAKES THE FORM OF AN OTTER.

11 INDIANA JONES, HERO OF THE POPULAR FILM SERIES OF THE SAME NAME, IS AFRAID OF SPIDERS.

12 THE COMIC BOOK HERO NAMED DAREDEVIL IS BLIND.

13 JODIE JENKINS IS THE HEROINE OF THE BOOK *THE STRONGEST GIRL IN THE WORLD*, BY SALLY GARDNER.

14 MARLIN, NEMO'S FATHER IN THE MOVIE *FINDING NEMO*, IS A MARLIN.

15 SUPERHERO THE FLASH CAN BEAT SUPERMAN IN A RACE.

16 FLINT, IN THE MOVIE *CLOUDY WITH A CHANCE OF MEATBALLS*, HAS A PET MONKEY NAMED DAVE.

17 SPIDER-MAN'S BLACK-AND-WHITE COSTUME WAS ONCE ACTUALLY AN ALIEN BEING.

18 OPTIMUS PRIME IS THE ROBOT LEADER OF THE DECEPTICONS IN THE TRANSFORMERS' TOY UNIVERSE.

19 ACCORDING TO HERMIONE GRANGER, FRIENDSHIP AND BRAVERY ARE MORE IMPORTANT THAN BOOKS AND CLEVERNESS.

20 THE DEVICE THAT GIVES TV HERO BEN 10 HIS POWER IS CALLED THE OMNITRIX.

21 FOLK HERO CASEY JONES WAS BEST KNOWN FOR BUILDING BRIDGES.

22 SUPERHERO OLIVER QUEEN, ALSO KNOWN AS GREEN ARROW, IS A BILLIONAIRE.

23 INDIANA JONES WAS NAMED AFTER A DOG THAT DIRECTOR GEORGE LUCAS ONCE OWNED.

24 IN THE BOOKS WRITTEN AFTER THE *STAR WARS* MOVIES, PRINCESS LEIA ORGANA SOLO IS A JEDI KNIGHT.

25 METAL-CLAWED COMIC BOOK SUPERHERO WOLVERINE IS ALMOST 100 YEARS OLD.

26 CLASSIC TV COWBOY THE LONE RANGER HAS A HORSE NAMED TONTO.

27 BILBO BAGGINS, FROM *THE HOBBIT*, FINDS A MAGICAL RING THAT ALLOWS HIM TO FLY.

28 COMIC BOOK CHARACTER BARBARA GORDON WAS BATGIRL BEFORE SHE WAS PARALYZED IN A FIGHT WITH THE JOKER.

29 THE MAIN HEROES OF THE TV SHOW *ADVENTURE TIME* ARE NAMED FINN AND JAKE.

30 THE SUPERHERO SHE-HULK IS THE SISTER OF THE INCREDIBLE HULK.

CHECK YOUR ANSWERS ON PAGES 167–168.

GAME SHOW

ULTIMATE POP CULTURE CHALLENGE

1 What year was the Etch A Sketch toy released?

a. 1776
b. 1865
c. 1959
d. 2000

2 "Poker Face," "Just Dance," and "Paparazzi" are songs from which pop star's debut album?

a. Lady Gaga
b. Adele
c. Selena Gomez
d. Katy Perry

3 In *The Penderwicks* book series, which of these characters is the youngest Penderwick daughter?

a. Batty Penderwick
b. Jane Penderwick
c. Skye Penderwick
d. Rosalind Penderwick

4 The character Cat from the TV show *Sam & Cat* was once a member of which other show?

a. *Jessie*
b. *Big Time Rush*
c. *iCarly*
d. *Victorious*

5 Which is the name of Grunkle Stan's business on the show *Gravity Falls*?

a. the Time Machine
b. the Mystery Shack
c. the Money Pit
d. the Wonder Museum

6 TRUE OR FALSE?
The Lightning Thief is the first title in the Heroes of Olympus book series.

7 The performer Psy became a hit on YouTube with which song?

a. "Psy Time"
b. "Pony Style"
c. "Gangnam Style"
d. "No Style"

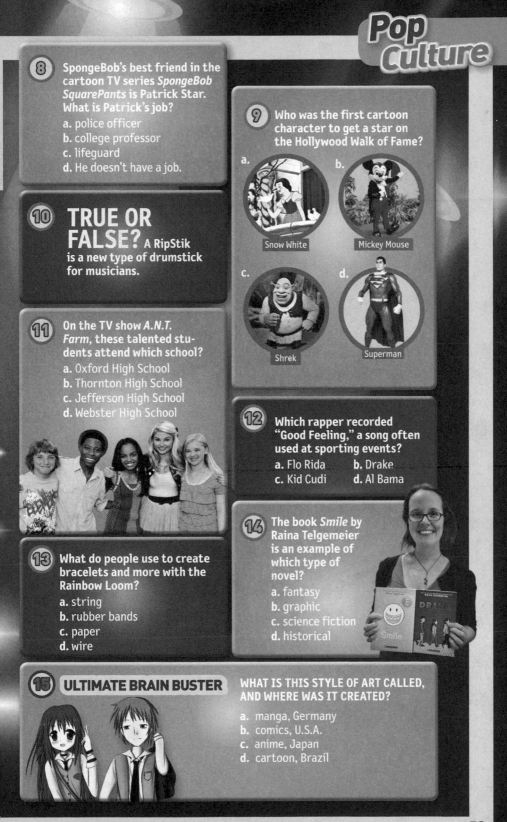

8 SpongeBob's best friend in the cartoon TV series *SpongeBob SquarePants* is Patrick Star. What is Patrick's job?
a. police officer
b. college professor
c. lifeguard
d. He doesn't have a job.

10 **TRUE OR FALSE?** A RipStik is a new type of drumstick for musicians.

11 On the TV show *A.N.T. Farm,* these talented students attend which school?
a. Oxford High School
b. Thornton High School
c. Jefferson High School
d. Webster High School

9 Who was the first cartoon character to get a star on the Hollywood Walk of Fame?

a. Snow White
b. Mickey Mouse
c. Shrek
d. Superman

12 Which rapper recorded "Good Feeling," a song often used at sporting events?
a. Flo Rida   b. Drake
c. Kid Cudi   d. Al Bama

14 The book *Smile* by Raina Telgemeier is an example of which type of novel?
a. fantasy
b. graphic
c. science fiction
d. historical

13 What do people use to create bracelets and more with the Rainbow Loom?
a. string
b. rubber bands
c. paper
d. wire

15 **ULTIMATE BRAIN BUSTER** WHAT IS THIS STYLE OF ART CALLED, AND WHERE WAS IT CREATED?
a. manga, Germany
b. comics, U.S.A.
c. anime, Japan
d. cartoon, Brazil

CHECK YOUR ANSWERS ON PAGES 167–168.

Wild WORLD

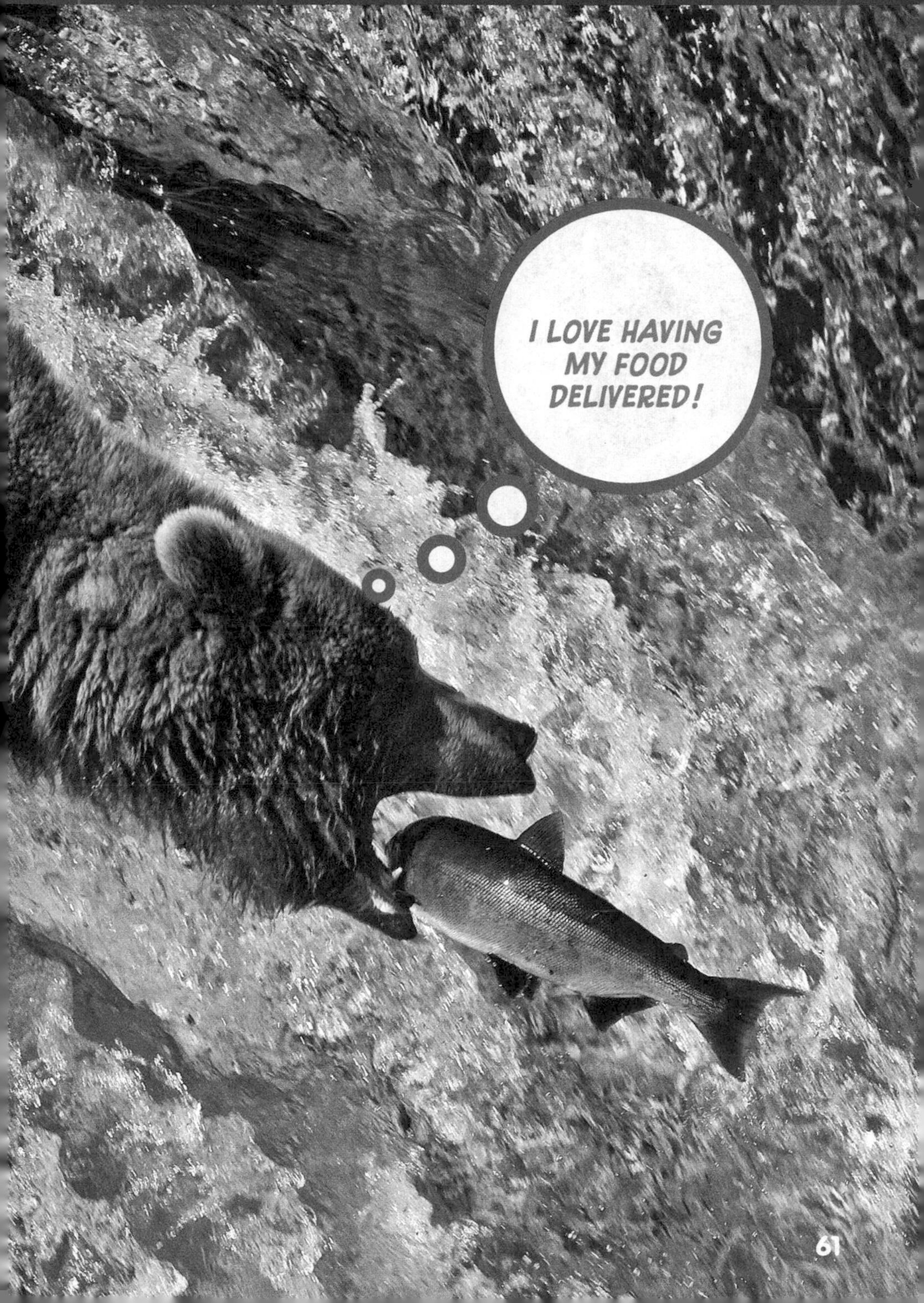
I LOVE HAVING MY FOOD DELIVERED!

Untamed!

1 Which flightless bird from New Zealand shares its name with a fruit?

a. an orange warbler
b. a kiwi
c. a white-winged mango
d. a fig

2 **True or false?** A small, nocturnal Asian primate called a tarsier is able to rotate its head 180 degrees.

TARSIER

3 Rodents are the single largest group of mammals. What trait do these animals all share?

a. rear digging claws
b. a long bushy tail
c. a single pair of incisors in the top and bottom jaw
d. webbed feet with claws for digging

4 **True or false?** Only male mosquitoes bite humans.

5 Which of the following is NOT a name for a polar bear?

a. Hairy Uncle Bear
b. Sea Bear
c. Old Man in the Fur Cloak
d. Ice Bear

6 Scientists have discovered that birds dream about _____.

a. cats
b. songs
c. nest building
d. auditioning for *American Idol*

GIRAFFE

7 **True or false?** Humans and giraffes have the same number of neck vertebrae.

BIG-EARED BAT

8 **What does a big-eared bat do with its ears when hibernating?**
a. coils them like rams' horns
b. folds them into thirds
c. sheds them like a snake's skin
d. chews on them for nourishment

9 **The sun bear gets its name from which distinctive feature?**
a. a tattoolike outline of the sun on its forehead
b. bright yellow eyes
c. a golden or white patch on its chest
d. pale yellow ears that are hot to the touch

BACTRIAN CAMEL

10 **How much can a thirsty Bactrian camel drink at one time?**
a. 2 gallons (7.5 L)
b. 30 gallons (113 L)
c. 75 gallons (254 L)
d. Bactrian camels do not drink water.

11 **What is the group name for a gathering of kangaroos?**
a. mob
b. suitcase
c. hopper
d. troop

KANGAROOS

CHECK YOUR ANSWERS ON PAGES 168–170.

PLANT PARTY

1 In the lifetime of a Venus flytrap, how many times can the trap open and close?

a. only once
b. exactly 2 times
c. about 3 or 4
d. more than 50

2 True or false? Hollow baobab trees have been used as a shop, prison, house, storage barn, and even a bus shelter.

3 In order to protect themselves from insects, some trees can _____.

a. turn invisible
b. send chemicals through the air to communicate with each other
c. move to another spot
d. turn into a different kind of tree

4 Which of the following plants shoots its seeds from its pods?

a. witch hazel
b. buttercup
c. flaming arrow shrub
d. daisy

5 What custom is most associated with the mistletoe plant?

a. using the leaves to make firecrackers
b. hiding it for others to find
c. kissing under it
d. using it for a piñata

6 According to legend, which plant keeps werewolves away?

a. marshmallow shrub
b. wolfsbane
c. English ivy
d. yellow wolf away

7 In the *Harry Potter* series, the Mandrake plant is deadly to anyone who _____.

a. eats its fruit
b. hears its scream
c. says its name aloud
d. smells it

8 True or false? One of the world's most expensive foods is a fungus.

9 Which ice-cream flavor is made from a pod on the flowering orchid?

a. chocolate   b. tutti-frutti
c. vanilla   d. banana

10 True or false? Tomatoes are poisonous when they are green.

11 Which plant has been known to save people stranded in the desert?

a. balloon plant
b. tumbleweed
c. water fountain fern
d. cactus

HOUSEFLY IN
VENUS FLYTRAP

CHECK YOUR ANSWERS ON PAGES 168–170.

Off the DEEP END

1 Tubeworms living near superhot vents eat what to survive?

   a. crabs boiled by the vents
   b. giant squid attracted to the vents
   c. poisonous gas spewing from the vents
   d. Krabby Patties from the nearest Krusty Krab

BLOBFISH

2 **True or false?** The blobfish, found at depths of more than 3,000 feet (914.4 m), has been voted the world's ugliest endangered creature.

3 Which of these is on the ocean floor and spans the entire planet?

   a. an underwater mountain range
   b. a very deep trench
   c. a coral reef
   d. a chain of starfish holding hands

4 If you were at the deepest point of the ocean, the weight of the water pushing down on you would feel most like _____.

   a. a person
   b. a car
   c. an airplane
   d. 50 airplanes

5 Besides making movies, James Cameron is also famous for doing what in the *DEEP SEA CHALLENGER* submersible?

   a. traveling to the ocean's darkest spot
   b. diving to the ocean's deepest point
   c. swimming in the coldest part of the ocean
   d. building the first underwater movie theater

DEEP SEA CHALLENGER

6 **True or false?** Cold salt water melting from sea ice can sink to the bottom of the ocean floor, creating a giant icicle as it sinks.

7 Spider crabs living on the ocean floor can grow up to how wide?
a. 1 foot (.3 m)
b. 3 feet (.9 m)
c. 12 feet (3.6 m)
d. 20 feet (6 m)

SPIDER CRAB

8 Scientists were shocked to discover that life on the ocean floor could exist without _____.
a. oxygen
b. food
c. gravity
d. Internet access

9 What did scientists discover on the ocean floor 1,000 miles (1,600 km) east of Japan?
a. the world's deepest canyon
b. the world's largest volcano
c. the world's tallest mountain
d. the world's largest Godzilla footprint

10 A deep-sea jellyfish will use flashy lights when attacked by a fish in order to _____.
a. scare the fish
b. blind the fish
c. attract a predator to eat the fish
d. convince the fish it was a lightbulb

11 What is the name given to the deepest part of the ocean?
a. Bikini Bottom
b. Mariana Trench
c. Champion Deep
d. Davy Jones's Locker

HELMET JELLY

CHECK YOUR ANSWERS ON PAGES 168–170.

CITY CRITTERS

1 Which wild animal can be found in more and more areas where people live?

a. coyote
b. leopard
c. grizzly bear
d. werewolf

2 This creature, sometimes found in the kitchen late at night, is considered one of the world's oldest living insects.

a. ladybug
b. snail
c. cockroach
d. doodlebug

3 True or false? Diseases spread by rats have killed more people than all human wars combined.

4 In New Delhi, India, which animals can be found in the streets, climbing on subways, and sneaking into homes?

a. rhesus monkeys   b. elephants
c. flamingos   d. wild dogs

5 The wild animals in the movie *Madagascar* escaped from which city zoo?

a. Safari Zoo, Berlin, Germany
b. Zimbabwe Wildlife Park, Africa
c. Central Park Zoo, New York, U.S.A.
d. Jardim Zoológico, Brazil

6 Which of these creatures is sometimes called a "rat with wings"?

a. guinea pig   b. mosquito
c. Monarch butterfly   d. pigeon

7 True or false? Raccoons, often found foraging in urban garbage cans, wash their food if they think it is dirty.

8 People in Moscow should be aware of this trick that some dogs on the street use to swipe snacks.

a. The dogs run into houses looking for food.
b. A dog barks to startle someone eating and then grabs his or her snack.
c. The dogs buy stolen credit cards.
d. all of the above

9 Why do urban birdwatchers claim that football stadiums can be a good site to watch birds?

a. Moths under the lights create a feeding frenzy for birds.
b. Birds are attracted to colorful uniforms.
c. Hot dogs and popcorn attract birds.
d. Birds can get discount tickets after halftime.

10 In 2012, a man in New York, U.S.A., was surprised to discover a 4-foot (1.2-m)-long California Kingsnake looking up at him from his

_____.

a. recliner   b. toilet
c. boot   d. picnic basket

11 In 2012, Chicago replaced Cincinnati, U.S.A., as the city most plagued by which pest?

a. alligators   b. bedbugs
c. goldfish   d. mosquitoes

ANTARCTIC CHILL!

1 How many sunrises does the South Pole experience each year?

a. none
b. 1
c. 4 (one each season)
d. 12 (one each month)

2 What is the coldest recorded temperature at the South Pole?

a. 32°F (0°C)
b. 2°F (−16.7°C)
c. −28°F (−33.33°C)
d. −117°F (−82.8°C)

3 Which is true about the South Pole?

a. It is the warmer of the two Poles.
b. The North Pole and South Pole experience the same temperatures.
c. It is the colder of the two Poles.
d. It is only cold during the summer.

4 What percentage of Antarctica is not covered in ice?

a. 2%
b. 20%
c. 50%
d. 100%

5 True or false? Because of Antarctica's location, winds are nonexistent on the continent.

6 What percent of the world's ice is found in the Antarctic ice sheet?

a. 2%
b. 15%
c. 65%
d. 90%

7 What is the average thickness of the ice sheet covering Antarctica?

a. 10 feet (3 m)
b. 50 feet (15.2 m)
c. 1.5 miles (2.4 km)
d. 30.5 miles (49 km)

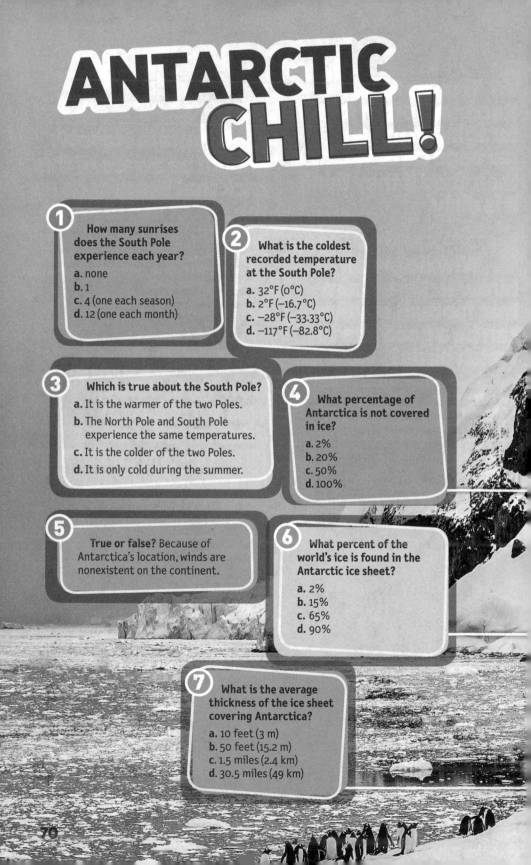

8 Which word best describes the ecosystem at the South Pole?
a. tropical rain forest
b. tundra
c. desert
d. savanna

9 True or false? Coal beds and fossils lead scientists to believe that Antarctica was once a warm place where trees and large animals lived.

10 How far does the South Pole drift each year?
a. It doesn't move at all.
b. less than 1 foot (30.5 cm)
c. 3.5 feet (1 m)
d. 20 feet (6.1 m)

11 Which of these animals does NOT live in Antarctica?
a. snow leopards
b. Adélie penguins
c. leopard seals
d. orcas

CHECK YOUR ANSWERS ON PAGES 168–170.

EQUATOR NAVIGATOR

1 **What covered Earth's Equator about 716 million years ago?**

a. weeds
b. hot lava
c. coffee beans
d. ice

2 **True or false?** Locations along the Equator experience the slowest sunrises and sunsets on the planet.

3 **Which is a myth that has often been told about life below the Equator?**

a. Everyone is left-handed.
b. Nobody sees a full moon.
c. Water flows down a drain clockwise (the opposite of how it flows above the Equator).
d. Shadows appear on the opposite side.

4 **What causes the bulge in the middle of Earth?**

a. the weight of people and animals that live near the Equator
b. the force created as Earth spins on its axis
c. heavy ice at the Poles
d. oceans near the Equator

5 **True or false?** People who are standing near the Equator move faster than people standing on the North or South Pole.

6 **Why is the area near the Equator the best place for space launches?**

a. Weather at the Equator is usually better for a space launch.
b. Cost for rocket fuel is less near the Equator.
c. The Earth's curve makes it easier to see the spacecraft take off.
d. Gravity is slightly weaker there.

7 Which of the following countries does the Equator NOT pass through?

a. Ecuador
b. France
c. Indonesia
d. Uganda

8 Which kind of animal can be found living both at the Equator and in Antarctica?

a. bear
b. rabbit
c. penguin
d. lion

9 Which aggressive rain forest creatures march in millions and eat anything that gets in their path?

a. spiny lizards
b. driver ants
c. crocodiles
d. moths

10 True or false? All climates around the Equator can be described as hot and humid.

11 Sailors who cross the Equator for the first time often celebrate the event. They are called _____ before they cross and _____ after they cross.

a. goldfish, sharks
b. pollywogs, shellbacks
c. puppies, dogs
d. onions, apples

12 Which fact is true about the Congo River in central and western Africa?

a. It is a longer river than the Nile.
b. It crosses the Equator twice on its way to the sea.
c. It runs all the way to Europe.
d. It is the only place to hear a style of music called "Congo Bongo."

CHECK YOUR ANSWERS ON PAGES 168–170.

MAP MANIA!
NATURE MAKES ITS MARK!

① ARCHES NATIONAL PARK

Which of the following helped form the natural arches in the western United States?

a. water, ice, wind
b. earthquakes and tsunamis
c. volcanoes
d. dinosaur soccer tournaments

NORTH AMERICA

ATLANTIC OCEAN

PACIFIC OCEAN

SOUTH AMERICA

② QUEEN'S HEAD

Formed over thousands of years due to erosion by the sea in Taiwan, this natural landmark is named for _____.

a. the queen chess piece
b. the Red Queen
c. England's Queen Elizabeth
d. *Alice in Wonderland's* Queen of Hearts

③ OLD FAITHFUL

True or false? The geyser called Old Faithful in Yellowstone National Park in Wyoming, U.S.A., was so named due to its predictable eruption every 5 minutes.

④ CAVE OF CRYSTALS

A cave of crystals was discovered below the Chihuahuan Desert in Mexico. The crystals are made from what?

a. diamonds
b. gypsum
c. desert sand
d. Chihuahuas

These landmarks are found around the world. Test your natural knowledge about each fantastic find, and then match each one to the correct location on the map.

Wild WORLD

5 QUINTANA ROO

Beneath the jungles of the Yucatán Peninsula, divers and explorers are drawn to what unique feature about Quintana Roo?

a. the world's longest underwater cave system

b. the world's warmest hot spring

c. the world's most populated fish habitat

d. the world's longest water slide

6 IGUAZU FALLS

This spectacular South American waterfall is actually made up of how many other, smaller waterfalls?

a. fewer than 20

b. between 25 and 50

c. approximately 100

d. more than 250

7 SHARK BAY

Rocklike structures known as stromatolites are similar to life-forms found on Earth more than a billion years ago! These living fossils off the coast of Australia were formed by _____.

a. sea dragons

b. scuba divers

c. blue-green algae

d. shark droppings

ARCTIC OCEAN

EUROPE

ASIA

AFRICA

B

PACIFIC OCEAN

INDIAN OCEAN

F.

ANTARCTICA

8–14

MATCH EACH LANDMARK TO THE RED MARKER ON THE MAP THAT SHOWS ITS CORRECT LOCATION.

Destination: Wild Side!

1 THERE ARE NO ACTIVE VOLCANOES IN ANTARCTICA.

2 THE DEEPEST KNOWN CAVE ON EARTH IS IN EASTERN EUROPE.

3 PEOPLE IN ICELAND SOMETIMES SEE POLAR BEARS WANDERING AROUND.

4 THE GREAT BARRIER REEF IS LOCATED OFF THE COAST OF ALASKA.

5 THE WORLD'S LARGEST BAMBOO PLANT IS IN JAPAN.

6 THE DEAD SEA OF ISRAEL AND JORDAN SUPPLIES DRINKING WATER FOR TWO COUNTRIES.

7 EGG-LAYING MAMMALS CAN BE FOUND ONLY IN AUSTRALIA.

8 MOUNTAINS COVER ROUGHLY HALF OF CHILE.

9 THE APPALACHIAN TRAIL RUNS ALONG THE WEST COAST OF THE UNITED STATES.

10 INDIA IS THE ONLY COUNTRY IN THE WORLD WHERE YOU CAN FIND BOTH LIONS AND TIGERS.

11 THERE IS A SWAMP IN RUSSIA THAT IS WIDER THAN THE COUNTRY OF SWITZERLAND.

12 SOUTH AFRICA HAS MORE VOLCANOES THAN ANY OTHER COUNTRY.

13 THE LOWEST POINT IN THE UNITED STATES IS DEATH VALLEY IN THE CALIFORNIA DESERT.

14 MORE THAN 6,000 KINDS OF PLANTS CAN BE FOUND IN JUST ONE 250-ACRE (100-HECTARE) AREA OF THE AMAZON RAIN FOREST IN PERU.

15 AT THE MASAI MARA NATIONAL RESERVE IN KENYA AND TANZANIA, TOURISTS CAN SEE THE "BIG FIVE": LIONS, ELEPHANTS, RHINOS, LEOPARDS, AND CAPE BUFFALO.

16 NORTH DAKOTA IS FARTHER FROM A COASTLINE THAN ANY OTHER PLACE IN NORTH AMERICA.

17 CANADA IS HOME TO THE PLANET'S LARGEST COASTAL TEMPERATE RAIN FOREST.

18 THE HOTTEST TEMPERATURE EVER RECORDED WAS RECORDED IN AFRICA.

19 THE NILE RIVER HAS TWO BRANCHES CALLED THE BLUE NILE AND THE PINK NILE.

20 THE GALÁPAGOS ISLANDS ARE HOME TO THE WORLD'S SMALLEST TURTLE SPECIES.

21 ALMOST 70 PERCENT OF THE LAND IN SWEDEN IS COVERED IN FORESTS.

22 THE COUNTRY OF MONGOLIA IS ONE OF THE COLDEST PLACES IN ASIA.

23 BOTSWANA IS ONE OF THE WORLD'S LARGEST DIAMOND PRODUCERS.

24 THE SALTIEST BODY OF WATER ON EARTH IS LOCATED IN EUROPE.

25 MOUNT OLYMPUS IN GREECE IS FAMOUS BECAUSE IT'S A POPULAR ROCK-CLIMBING SPOT.

26 THE LARGEST GLACIER IN THE WORLD COVERS OVER 3.8 MILLION SQUARE MILES (1 MILLION SQ. KM).

27 TO VISIT THE SILENT STONE FIGURES OF EASTER ISLAND, YOU WOULD TRAVEL TO THE UNITED KINGDOM.

28 VICTORIA FALLS IN AFRICA IS ABOUT TWICE AS TALL AS NIAGARA FALLS, ON THE BORDER OF THE U.S.A. AND CANADA.

29 A PORTION OF THE ANDES MOUNTAINS FORMS THE BORDER BETWEEN ARGENTINA AND CHILE.

30 AFRICA'S SERENGETI HOSTS MILLIONS OF WILD ANIMALS.

CHECK YOUR ANSWERS ON PAGES 168–170.

Out of THIS WORLD!

1 Earth is the third planet from the Sun and is _____ in the solar system in terms of size.
- **a.** first
- **b.** fourth
- **c.** fifth
- **d.** seventh

2 Which planet has several moons, including a volcanic moon and an icy moon?
- **a.** Mercury
- **b.** Earth
- **c.** Jupiter
- **d.** Venus

3 The biggest canyon in the solar system can be found on which planet?
- **a.** Mars
- **b.** Earth
- **c.** Venus
- **d.** Neptune

MARINER VALLEY

4 To see a sunrise on this planet, you'd need to look west instead of east.
- **a.** Venus
- **b.** Earth
- **c.** Mars
- **d.** Saturn

5 True or false? The Romans named the planet Mercury because they believed it contained large deposits of mercury.

SATURN

6 As this planet enters its spring season, it experiences storms the size of North America.
- **a.** Mercury
- **b.** Venus
- **c.** Uranus
- **d.** Only Earth experiences seasons.

78

THUNDERSTORM

7 **True or false?** As Earth spins on its axis, it wobbles like a spinning top.

8 **Which of the following is the only object in the solar system larger than Jupiter?**

a. Mars
b. Jabba the Hut
c. Earth
d. the sun

MILKY WAY

9 **In terms of size and composition, which planet is considered a near twin of Earth?**

a. Venus
b. Neptune
c. Mars
d. Uranus

10 **It is estimated that the Milky Way galaxy contains how many suns?**

a. only 1
b. 30 to 50
c. over 500,000
d. over one hundred billion

11 **What is the approximate total weight of cosmic dust that falls to Earth each day?**

a. 50,000 pounds (22,679.6 kg)
b. 1 ton (907 kg)
c. 20 tons (18,143 kg)
d. 40,000 tons (36,287,390 kg)

COSMIC DUST

WINDY WEATHER

1 The swirling winds of dust or sand, often called a dust devil in the United States, is known as what in Australia?

a. up-and-down
b. whirly-whirly
c. blustery-dusty
d. sand tower

2 The Tornado Super Outbreak of 2011 in the U.S.A. was the largest outbreak of tornadoes ever recorded, with more than _____ tornadoes striking 15 states.

a. 25　　　　b. 100
c. 150　　　 d. 300

3 True or false? Mars experiences tornado-like dust storms that can cover the entire planet in dust.

4 "Cyclone" and "typhoon" are two names for what type of storm?

a. lightning　　b. hurricane
c. blizzard　　 d. sandstorm

5 What is one way to keep sand dunes from moving when the wind blows?

a. Build a shed around them.
b. Grow plants on top of them.
c. Pour water on them.
d. Nothing. They are too heavy to blow away.

6 *Derecho* is a rapidly moving windstorm and comes from the Spanish word that means _____.

a. destructive
b. windy
c. straight
d. westerly

7 Which continent has the windiest coasts in the world?

a. Antarctica
b. Australia
c. Europe
d. North America

8 True or false? The fastest wind speed ever recorded occurred during a tornado.

9 A simoom is an extremely dry and hot wind that can reach temperatures of about 130°F (55°C). It gets its name from the Arabic word that means what?

a. poison
b. hot soup
c. wind of the sun
d. blowing heat

10 The first known windmill that created electrical power was built in Scotland in which year?

a. 1200
b. 1607
c. 1887
d. 1975

11 In 2005, what rained down on a small town in Serbia during a period of high winds?

a. dolphins
b. school supplies
c. fruits and vegetables
d. thousands of frogs

12 True or false? Wildfires can create rotating winds that result in tornadoes made of fire.

GAME SHOW

ULTIMATE WILD WORLD CHALLENGE

1 Sailors in the 1500s often claimed to see "sea monsters" that scientists today think were what?
a. rocks in the ocean
b. giant squid
c. mermaids
d. the sailors' reflection in the water

2 The giant, carnivorous pitcher plant, found in the Philippines, attracts what unsuspecting prey?
a. rodents
b. goats
c. water buffaloes
d. Bengal tigers

3 The Southern Elephant Seal weighs as much as _____.
a. a bicycle
b. two cars
c. a digital clock
d. the Statue of Liberty

4 Scientists based the pirate ant's name on what unique feature?
a. It has a wooden leg.
b. It has dark-colored eye patches.
c. It lives only on ships, not on land.
d. It walks across every plank it finds.

5 What is the name given to the polar robot that scientists believe will greatly improve the safety of exploration at the North and South Poles?
a. R2D2
b. the Abominable Snowman
c. Yeti
d. Fred Flintstone

6 If you're a lion in Tanzania, when is your favorite time at night to hunt?
a. when the moon is shining
b. when the moon is below the horizon and cannot be seen
c. only during a full moon
d. anytime the pizza place won't deliver an extra-large antelope with cheese

7 TRUE OR FALSE?
When local flooding caused wolf spiders to head for higher ground, the spiders left the town of Wagga Wagga, Australia, covered in spider silk.

8 Believed to be the largest freshwater species on Earth, giant stingrays are found where?
a. in a backyard swimming pool
b. in Cambodia's Mekong River
c. off the coast of Florida, U.S.A.
d. at an aquarium

9 Known as the prairie in the U.S.A. and savannas in Africa, what are these grasslands called in South America?
a. pampas
b. wheat fields
c. tundra
d. desert

11 TRUE OR FALSE?
The mother of U.S. President Abraham Lincoln died after drinking milk from a cow that had eaten a poisonous plant.

10 Scientists believe the sugar palm tree can help people living in rain forests. Why?
a. It scares away tigers.
b. It can help make biofuels.
c. It looks good in a garden.
d. It makes a good tree for tree houses.

13 What is the name given to this unusual rock formation found in Wyoming, U.S.A.?
a. Devil's Tower
b. Tree Trunk Mountain
c. Giant's Ankle
d. Rock Mountain Number 3

12 What causes most avalanches?
a. winds above 150 miles an hour (241 km/h)
b. earthquakes
c. snowshoe rabbits
d. people

15 ULTIMATE BRAIN BUSTER
Which of these animals would most likely NOT be found in a tundra, a large plain without trees in the Arctic regions?

a. mountain goat
b. caribou
c. platypus
d. snow goose

14 TRUE OR FALSE?
Deserts can be found on every continent except Asia.

Olympic Fever!

1 **With professional basketball stars Michael Jordan, Larry Bird, and Magic Johnson on the roster, the 1992 American men's Olympic basketball team was called _____.**

a. the Golden Boys
b. the Ol' Timers
c. the Unbeatables
d. the Dream Team

2 **The oldest competitor in Olympic history was Oscar Swahn of Sweden, who was 72 years, 281 days old at the 1920 Olympics. In which sport did Swahn compete?**

a. shooting   b. rowing
c. equestrian   d. gymnastics

3 **True or False? The first Olympic champion on record was a Greek soldier who won the weight-lifting competition.**

4 **To make sure athletes had the best possible conditions, officials at the 1980 Winter Games in New York, U.S.A., did what?**

a. started competitions late in the afternoons
b. used artificial snow
c. provided each athlete with peanut butter and jelly sandwiches
d. canceled competitions on cloudy days

5 **Which female athlete won the most gold medals of any woman at the 2012 Summer Olympic Games in London, England?**

a. McKayla Maroney
b. Ye Shiwen

6
Which country's athletes are the first to enter the stadium during the opening ceremonies for the Olympic Games?

a. U.S.A.
b. China
c. Afghanistan
d. Greece

7
Which object is carried from Olympia, Greece, to the location of each Olympic Games?

a. a symbolic gyro
b. a flame torch
c. a gold medal
d. an olive wreath

8
American swimmer Johnny Weissmuller won a total of five gold medals in the 1924 and 1928 Olympic Games before playing which famous movie character?

a. Superman
b. Sherlock Holmes
c. Tarzan
d. Aquaman

9
This *Dancing With the Stars* winner also has won the most Winter Olympics medals of any American.

a. Bonnie Blair
b. Mark Spitz
c. Michelle Kwan
d. Apolo Anton Ohno

10
Which of the following mascots paraded around the 2012 London Summer Olympic Games?

a. Misha and Sasha
b. Wenlock and Mandeville
c. Moe, Larry, and Curly
d. Quatchi and Miga

CHECK YOUR ANSWERS ON PAGES 170–171.

TRUE or FALSE?

Sports Kickoffs

1 THE ORIGINS OF THE ENGLISH BAT-AND-BALL SPORT KNOWN AS CRICKET DATE TO THE 13TH CENTURY.

2 VOLLEYBALL WAS FIRST PLAYED BY BUSINESSPEOPLE WHO COULD NOT HANDLE THE ROUGHNESS OF BASKETBALL.

3 A BOOK WRITTEN IN 1744 OUTLINED THE OFFICIAL RULES OF BASEBALL.

4 NASCAR IS A SHORTENED NAME FOR NATIONAL ASSOCIATION OF SPECIAL CARS AND RACERS.

5 ENGLISH NOBILITY DEVELOPED THE SPORT OF HORSERACING.

6 AMERICAN FOOTBALL COMBINES ELEMENTS OF ICE HOCKEY AND ENGLISH FOOTBALL.

7 IN THE FIRST GAME OF BASKETBALL, PLAYERS TOSSED THE BALL INTO PEACH BASKETS RATHER THAN HOOPS.

8 THE SPORT OF SOCCER WAS GIVEN ITS NAME BECAUSE PLAYERS "SOCK" THE BALL WITH THEIR FEET.

9 THE OLDEST-KNOWN SNOW SKIS ARE BELIEVED TO BE BETWEEN 9,000 AND 10,000 YEARS OLD.

10 RUGBY GOT ITS NAME BECAUSE IT HELPED THE PLAYERS DEVELOP THEIR RUGGEDNESS.

11 FRENCH EMPEROR NAPOLEON BONAPARTE INVENTED THE SPORT OF COMPETITIVE ICE-SKATING.

12 BEFORE IT BECAME A POPULAR SPORT, SURFING WAS ONCE BANNED IN HAWAII.

13 THE ORIGINS OF ICE HOCKEY GO BACK TO A GAME PLAYED BY NATIVE AMERICANS LIVING IN NOVA SCOTIA, CANADA.

14 IN EARLY AMERICAN FOOTBALL GAMES, TEAMS WERE AWARDED FIVE POINTS FOR A FIELD GOAL.

15 WHEN SOFTBALL FIRST STARTED, ANOTHER NAME FOR THE GAME IN THE U.S.A. WAS "KITTEN BALL."

16 THE ANCIENT EGYPTIANS PLAYED A SPORT SIMILAR TO BOWLING.

17 TONY HAWK INVENTED THE SKATEBOARD.

18 DURING SOME EARLY BICYCLE RACES IN THE 1800S, RIDERS HAD TO WALK THEIR BIKES UP STEEP HILLS.

19 TENNIS STARTED OUT AS A FRENCH HANDBALL GAME CALLED *JEU DE PAUME*, WHICH MEANS "GAME OF THE PALM."

20 BASKETBALL IS OFTEN DESCRIBED AS THE ONLY U.S.-INVENTED MAJOR SPORT, BUT ITS INVENTOR WAS CANADIAN.

21 IN THE SPORT OF CURLING, PLAYERS USE CURLING IRONS TO SLIDE STONES ACROSS A SHEET OF ICE TOWARD A TARGET.

22 THE CINCINNATI RED STOCKINGS WAS THE NAME OF THE FIRST PROFESSIONAL BASEBALL TEAM.

23 WEIGHT-LIFTING COMPETITIONS TRACE THEIR ORIGINS BACK TO STRONGMEN WHO PERFORMED IN CIRCUSES AND THEATERS.

24 THE MARTIAL ART KUNG FU WAS INVENTED IN JAPAN.

25 SKI JUMPING IS A RELATIVELY NEW SPORT.

26 EARLY HOCKEY GAMES ALLOWED AS MANY AS 30 PLAYERS FROM EACH TEAM ON THE ICE.

27 BEFORE VOLLEYBALLS WERE INVENTED, VOLLEYBALL GAMES WERE PLAYED WITH BASKETBALLS.

28 WHEN TENNIS WAS FIRST PLAYED, IT WAS KNOWN AS "GRASS TENNIS" BECAUSE IT WAS PLAYED ON GRASS COURTS.

29 THE FIRST KENTUCKY DERBY RACES WERE HELD IN THE DOWNTOWN AREA OF LOUISVILLE, KENTUCKY.

30 NATIVE AMERICAN LACROSSE GAMES WERE SOMETIMES PLAYED WITH GOALS SET MILES APART.

CHECK YOUR ANSWERS ON PAGES 170–171.

Fields of Dreams

1 SKI DUBAI

This hot desert country is home to the indoor Ski Dubai resort, which houses a snow-covered hill that is 25 stories high.

a. United Arab Emirates
b. South Africa
c. Mexico
d. Saudi Arabia

2 ROMAN COLOSSEUM

In addition to gladiator battles, the Colosseum in Rome, Italy, was flooded on purpose so spectators could watch which type of events?

a. swimming competitions
b. fishing competitions
c. water-ski shows
d. mock naval battles

3 COWBOYS STADIUM

True or False?
The total weight of the giant video board that hangs from the roof of Cowboys Stadium in Dallas, Texas, U.S.A., is 1.2 million pounds (544,310 kg).

NORTH AMERICA

•G •E

ATLANTIC OCEAN

•D

SOUTH AMERICA

PACIFIC OCEAN

You'd have to travel the globe to visit all of these sporty venues. Take this quick tour to find out how much you know about these human-made marvels. Then try to match each one to the correct location on the map.

④ WIMBLEDON

Approximately how many tennis balls are used during the 13 days of the Wimbledon tennis tournament in London, England?

a. 500
b. 5,000
c. 50,000
d. 500,000

ARCTIC OCEAN

EUROPE

ASIA

AFRICA

INDIAN OCEAN

⑤ STADIO HERNANDO SILES

Built in the Andes Mountains of La Paz, Bolivia, Stadio Hernando Siles was once banned from hosting World Cup soccer because _____ .

a. the stadium's altitude was too high above sea level
b. the stadium's food services were not good enough
c. the playing surface tilted toward one goal
d. the fans were the craziest in the world

⑥ RUNGRADO MAY DAY STADIUM

With a seating capacity of 150,000, multipurpose Rungrado May Day Stadium in Pyongyang is the world's largest. In which country is this mammoth stadium located?

a. China
b. Japan
c. Australia
d. North Korea

⑦ CHURCHILL DOWNS

For more than 138 years, Churchill Downs, located in a southeastern state in the U.S.A, has been the home of which famous horse race?

a. the Churchill Challenge
b. the Kentucky Derby
c. the Belmont Stakes
d. the Pinewood Derby

8–14

MATCH EACH SPORTS VENUE TO THE RED MARKER ON THE MAP THAT SHOWS ITS CORRECT LOCATION.

FROM CHAMP TO CELEBRITY

1. For which Major League Baseball team did Bryce Harper win the 2012 National League Rookie of the Year award?

a. the Washington Nationals
b. the Capital Clubbers
c. the Miami Marlins
d. the Tampa Bay Rays

2. Super Bowl winner and football Hall of Famer John Madden is also the celebrity spokesperson for what?

a. *Monday Night Football*
b. Madden Country Buffet restaurants
c. *Madden NFL* video games
d. Madden recreational buses

3. True or False? Soccer star Neymar is the richest soccer player in the world.

NEYMAR

4. Washington Redskins quarterback Robert Griffin III is better known to football fans as _____.

a. Running Robert
b. RG-TD
c. Mia Hamm
d. RG3

5. Which athlete has won the most Nickelodeon Kids' Choice Awards for favorite female athlete?

a. Kristi Yamaguchi
b. Danica Patrick
c. Mia Hamm
d. Florence Griffith Joyner

6. In her first game with the Phoenix Mercury, Brittney Griner became the first woman to do what in a women's professional basketball game?

a. take over head coaching duties
b. dunk twice
c. get stuck in the net
d. foul out

KRISTI YAMAGUCHI

7 Gabby Douglas earned an individual gold medal at the 2012 Olympic Games in London, England, for which gymnastics competition?

a. all-around champion
b. pole vault
c. floor exercise
d. trampoline

GABBY DOUGLAS

8 **True or False?** Basketball legend Shaquille O'Neal once starred in a movie about a seven-foot-tall dancing dentist.

9 Lindsey Vonn's athletic accomplishments have earned her spots on TV and many product endorsements. Which sport does Vonn excel in?

a. tennis
b. competitive marble rolling
c. skiing
d. swimming

10 In 2012, Los Angeles Angels center fielder Mike Trout earned Major League Baseball All-Star Game honors and which American League award?

a. Newcomers Trophy
b. Rookie of the Year
c. Most Valuable Player
d. Cy Young Award

MIKE TROUT

11 **True or False?** Before he ever played in the NBA, LeBron James signed a deal with Nike worth $90 million.

LEBRON JAMES

12 Which country does golfing superstar Rory McIlroy call home?

a. England
b. Golfestan
c. Northern Ireland
d. U.S.A.

CHECK YOUR ANSWERS ON PAGES 170–171.

Record Setters

1 Soccer player Lionel Messi became the first to win four World Player of the Year awards. Which country does Messi come from?

a. Brazil
b. Argentina
c. Italy
d. Spain

2 Which baseball slugger hit his record-breaking 756th career home run in 2007 while playing for the San Francisco Giants?

a. Sammy Sosa
b. Babe Ruth
c. Mark McGwire
d. Barry Bonds

3 High school cheerleader Miranda Ferguson of Texas, U.S.A., performed 35 of these in a row in 2012.

a. jumping jacks
b. backward handsprings
c. push-ups
d. cartwheels

4 Wayne Gretzky holds or shares 61 records. In which sport did Gretzky become known as "The Great One"?

a. badminton
b. baseball
c. ice hockey
d. tennis

5 Miguel Indurain of Spain won the Tour de France a record five times. Which kind of competition is the Tour de France?

a. swimming
b. hiking
c. skiing
d. cycling

6 In which racing car series did Richard Petty win 200 races, the most of any driver?

a. NASCAR
b. FASTCAR
c. Indy Car Series
d. Formula One

7 Which American scored her 159th career international soccer goal in 2013, becoming the all-time leader?

a. Julie Foudy
b. Abby Wambach
c. Taylor Swift
d. Mia Hamm

8 Tom Brady set a National Football League record in 2007 by throwing 50 touchdown passes. For which team did Brady play?

a. Indianapolis Colts
b. New England Patriots
c. Chicago Bears
d. Denver Broncos

9 Which award did Greg Maddux win a record 18 times as the best fielding pitcher in baseball's National League?

a. the Good Hands Plaque
b. the Silver Spikes
c. the Gold Glove
d. the Lavender Leather Award

CHECK YOUR ANSWERS ON PAGES 170–171.

FAST, FURIOUS, AND FUN!

1 How quickly can a Formula One pit crew remove and install four tires?

a. 30 seconds
b. 1.9 seconds
c. 10.5 seconds
d. 1 minute

2 **True or False?** Formula One is the world's second most popular auto-racing series.

3 A driver's racing suit can protect against temperatures of 1544°F (840°C), which is about as hot as _____.

a. a hot summer's day
b. a campfire
c. lava from a volcanic eruption
d. a sauna

4 Formula One racing is also known by what other name?

a. stock car racing
b. NASCAR Europe
c. drag racing
d. grand prix racing

5 **True or False?** The word "formula" in Formula One refers to a special blend of gasoline the car uses.

6 The front and back wings on a car push it down onto the track as it races, which is an example of _____.

a. astronomy   b. chemistry
c. aerodynamics   d. hydroponics

FORMULA ONE RACE CAR

Sports Challenge

7 Except for the gas and brake pedals, almost all the controls a driver needs to race are located _____.

a. on the dashboard
b. near the driver's feet
c. on a joystick
d. on the steering wheel

8 Used energy from a Formula One car's brakes is captured by a special recovery system. How does the driver use this extra power?

a. to pass other cars
b. for more braking power
c. to go in reverse if needed
d. to make quicker bathroom stops

9 Antennae on a race car send information—in a process called telemetry—about the car's performance by way of which technologies?

a. smart phones and iPads
b. one-way radios and a racing app
c. onboard sensors and wireless communications
d. binoculars and telephones

10 In which country would you find the headquarters for the Ferrari Formula One racing team?

a. England
b. Germany
c. Japan
d. Italy

11 How quickly can a Formula One engine propel the car from 0 to 124 miles an hour (0 to 200 km/h)?

a. 1 second
b. 3.8 seconds
c. 10.7 seconds
d. 20.5 seconds

CHECK YOUR ANSWERS ON PAGES 170–171.

GEAR AND GARB

1 What is the largest basketball shoe size in NBA history?
- **a.** 13.5
- **b.** 22
- **c.** 30
- **d.** 16.5

2 High-tech bodysuits for competitive swimmers were banned in 2009 in part because they _____.
- **a.** help swimmers float
- **b.** have fins
- **c.** create too much water turbulence
- **d.** are too colorful

COMPETITIVE SWIMMERS

3 **True or False?** The equipment a hockey goalie uses in the NHL can weigh as much as 40 pounds (18.1 kg).

4 During the course of the Iditarod sled-dog race, mushers may use around 2,000 of which item?
- **a.** dog-feet booties
- **b.** tissue boxes
- **c.** tubes of lip balm
- **d.** pairs of socks

5 The special skateboards used in the sport of street luge can reach top speeds of _____.
- **a.** 150 mph (241 km/h)
- **b.** 55 mph (88 km/h)
- **c.** 25 mph (40 km/h)
- **d.** 80 mph (129 km/h)

STREET LUGER

6 The proper name for the uniform a wrestler must wear is a _____.

a. tightie-whitey
b. leotard
c. singlet
d. power suit

7 Rackets equipped with string dampeners are supposed to prevent which common tennis injury?

a. tennis toe
b. tennis shoulder
c. tennis elbow
d. tennis wrist

8 Which is the only color horse jockeys cannot wear on their racing silks or uniforms?

a. pea-soup green
b. navy blue
c. beige
d. white

9 **True or False?** The numbers on the backs of baseball uniforms were originally used to indicate the order in which players batted.

10 A boom, jib, and sloop rig are equipment used in which sport?

a. cycling
b. base jumping
c. boxing
d. sailing

11 How many footballs must the home team provide for an NFL game played outdoors?

a. 15
b. 3
c. 36
d. 1

CHECK YOUR ANSWERS ON PAGES 170–171.

The Soccer Scene

1 Which is a commonly used term to describe a soccer playing surface?

a. the yard
b. the pitch
c. the lawn
d. the square

2 True or False? A player penalized with a red card must sit out 10 minutes before reentering the game.

3 How often is the World Cup tournament held?

a. every 2 years
b. each leap year
c. every 10 years
d. every 4 years

4 When delivering a throw-in, a player must keep what on the ground?

a. at least one foot
b. the ball
c. a part of both feet
d. his or her knees

5 What is the name of the men's professional soccer league in North America?

a. the American Premier League (APL)
b. the World Organization of Professional Soccer (WOOPS)
c. the American Soccer League (ASL)
d. Major League Soccer (MLS)

6 True or False? Only the goalkeeper is allowed to touch the ball with his or her hands.

7 What are the two long boundary lines called that mark the sides of a soccer playing field?

a. no-no lines
b. sidelines
c. out-of-bounds lines
d. touch lines

8 Which player has played in a record 352 international soccer games?

a. Kristine Lilly
b. Mia Hamm
c. Landon Donovan
d. David Beckham

9 Players who are highly skilled at scoring goals should play which position?

a. defender
b. goalkeeper
c. forward
d. midfielder

10 During a soccer match, players in which position are likely to run the greatest distance?

a. goalkeepers
b. midfielders
c. defenders
d. forwards

11 What are the dimensions of a standard professional soccer goal?

a. 24 feet (7.3 m) wide and 8 feet (2.4 m) high
b. 20 feet (6.1 m) wide and 15 feet (4.6 m) high
c. 16 feet (4.9 m) wide and 6 feet (1.8 m) high
d. 8 feet (2.4 m) wide and 4 feet (1.2 m) high

12 In which country did professional soccer first develop?

a. Mexico
b. U.S.A.
c. Brazil
d. England

QUEST FOR GLORY

1 Which team has won the most Super Bowl titles?
- a. the New Orleans Saints
- b. the Miami Dolphins
- c. the Green Bay Packers
- d. the Pittsburgh Steelers

DREW BREES OF THE NEW ORLEANS SAINTS

2 What is the name of the hockey trophy that contains the names of the players, coaches, and team officials from the winning teams?
- a. the Sippy Cup
- b. the World Cup
- c. the Stanley Cup
- d. America's Cup

INDIANAPOLIS 500

3 Since 1936, winners of the Indianapolis 500 car race have celebrated on the victory stand by _____.
- a. saying, "I love you, Mom"
- b. drinking a bottle of milk
- c. showering the crowd with orange juice
- d. singing "Back Home Again in Indiana"

4 The Tour de France rider with the lowest cumulative time after each stage is awarded what?
- a. a yellow jersey
- b. French cheese
- c. a polka-dotted jersey
- d. a new bike

5 **True or False?** In 1966, the famous World Cup trophy was stolen in London, England, and recovered by Pickles, a mongrel dog.

WORLD CUP TROPHY

6 During the 1919 World Series, the Chicago White Sox performance earned them the nickname "The Black Sox" because _____.

a. they wore dirty socks
b. they intentionally lost the World Series
c. they often broke the rules
d. they used black bats

1919 CHICAGO WHITE SOX

7 **True or False?** The Los Angeles Lakers hold the record for the most championships in a row in all the major North American sports.

8 What is the name of the trophy annually awarded to the most outstanding college football player in the U.S.A.?

a. the Lady Byng Trophy
b. the George Gip Trophy
c. the Heisman Trophy
d. the Golden Ball

9 **True or False?** Each player on the team that wins the Stanley Cup gets to spend 24 hours with the trophy.

10 Which tennis player has won the most Wimbledon titles?

a. Pete Sampras
b. Sammy Wii
c. Serena Williams
d. Martina Navratilova

IRISH HURLERS

11 What kind of athletes are Masters champions?

a. tennis players
b. golfers
c. Irish hurlers
d. lawn bowlers

CHECK YOUR ANSWERS ON PAGES 170–171.

GAME SHOW

ULTIMATE
SPORTS CHALLENGE

1 Which driver has won the most races in Formula One history?
a. Sebastian Vettel
b. Goggles Pisano
c. Michael Schumacher
d. Mario Andretti

2 In which country were the first modern Olympic Games held in 1896?
a. France
b. U.S.A.
c. Greece
d. England

3 **TRUE OR FALSE?**

The America's Cup is one of the most famous trophies in sailing.

4 Which two sports did Brazilians combine to create *futevôlei*?
a. lacrosse and tennis
b. soccer and volleyball
c. baseball and Ping-Pong
d. rugby and volleyball

5 Which is the oldest baseball stadium in use in Major League Baseball?
a. Fenway Park
b. Yankee Stadium
c. Whoville Park
d. Wrigley Field

6 **TRUE OR FALSE?** Figure skating was given its name because skaters had to *figure* out which jumps and spins to perform.

7 Which sport is this athlete playing?
a. curling
b. rugby
c. lacrosse
d. cricket

8 What is a perfect score in a game of bowling?

a. 10
b. 100
c. 300
d. 500

9 The Ryder Cup is an international golf competition that began in 1927 featuring which two countries?

a. England and Scotland
b. England and U.S.A.
c. Japan and China
d. Canada and Russia

10 ## TRUE OR FALSE?

Snooker is a game that is similar to golf.

11 How many players make up an official indoor volleyball team?

a. 5
b. 10
c. 2
d. 6

12 What is the name of the equipment this gymnast is performing on?

a. the uneven parallel bars
b. the split-level gymnast bars
c. the spring bars
d. the Olympic parallel bars

13 According to baseball tradition, when do you hear a crowd sing "Take Me Out to the Ball Game"?

a. before the third inning hot dog rush
b. after the final out
c. during the seventh-inning stretch
d. between the fourth and fifth innings

14 Bob Beamon made a record leap of 29.2 feet (8.9 m) at the 1968 Summer Olympics in which event?

a. the standing broad jump
b. the long jump
c. the triple jump
d. the run, spin, jump

15 ## ULTIMATE BRAIN BUSTER

CAN YOU IDENTIFY THIS SOCCER STAR, WHO IS THOUGHT TO BE ONE OF THE BEST FORWARDS EVER TO PLAY THE GAME?

SAGRES

Fashion Forward

1. If you were wearing a "union suit" in the 1800s, which would you have on?
   a. matching shirt and pants
   b. a Civil War costume
   c. long underwear
   d. snorkel and fins

2. Which of the following is the oldest type of clothing item?
   a. toga
   b. hat
   c. skirt
   d. loincloth

3. Which did Levi Strauss get a patent to make in 1873?
   a. work boots
   b. tutus
   c. flannel shirts
   d. denim jeans

4. If you lived in the 1920s and saw a "flapper," what would you be looking at?
   a. a chicken suit
   b. a woman who dressed in a certain style
   c. an early version of a helicopter
   d. a pilot's outfit

5. A kimono is a fancy dress, often made from silk. Where was it first used?
   a. Japan
   b. Mexico
   c. Transylvania
   d. Egypt

6. **True or false?** Two thousand years ago, Roman citizens were not allowed to wear togas to gladiator combat games.

KIMONO

OLD-FASHIONED NECKTIE

7 In the 1800s, if you touched a man's necktie, which might happen next?

a. He would tell you his name.
b. He would tell you where he bought it.
c. He would challenge you to a duel.
d. He would show you how to tie it.

8 Stiff corsets under dresses were a popular fashion item in the mid-1800s. Which made the corsets so stiff?

a. bamboo
b. steel
c. magic
d. whale bones

9 When did the baseball cap make its first appearance?

a. 100 B.C.
b. 1790
c. 1860
d. 1950

10 True or false? Large white wigs are still worn sometimes by people in British government.

11 What is the name of this fashion style, which was popular during the 1980s?

a. clown
b. dandy
c. goth
d. hipster

12 Which of these was popular with women and girls starting in the 1960s?

a. go-go boots
b. saddle shoes
c. flip-flops
d. tap shoes

CHECK YOUR ANSWERS ON PAGES 172–173.

New in the 1990s

1 Which video game sensation started in the 1990s and featured characters such as Pikachu and Meowth?

a. Super Mario Brothers
b. Pokémon
c. Sonic the Hedgehog
d. Scribblenauts

2 True or false? The first female astronaut to pilot a space shuttle blasted off in 1995.

3 True or false? Clothes worn backward became a fashion trend for hip-hop fans during the 1990s.

4 In 1997, the Sojourner rover sent back the first images from the surface of which planet?

a. Jupiter
b. Venus
c. Mars
d. Krypton

5 Which popular 1990s television show was about a girl hero who was tough and strong?

a. *The Real World*
b. *Moesha*
c. *Sister, Sister*
d. *Buffy the Vampire Slayer*

6 Which clothing item did 1990s "grunge" music make popular?

a. skinny jeans
b. neckties
c. flannel shirts
d. yoga pants

7 In 1998, the popular *Legend of Zelda* video game series went 3-D for the first time in which adventure?

a. "Ocarina of Time"
b. "Princess Peach's Revenge"
c. "Link Takes a Vacation"
d. "Zelda Goes to College"

8 When a sheep named Dolly was born in 1996, she was considered a great scientific breakthrough because _____.

a. she could talk
b. she had been cloned
c. she had two heads
d. she became an astronaut

9 The Channel Tunnel, or Chunnel, is an underwater tunnel completed in 1994 that links which two countries?

a. England and France
b. Ireland and Wales
c. the U.S.A. and Cuba
d. Spain and Greece

10 True or false? Jay-Z starred in the 1990s television show *The Fresh Prince of Bel Air.*

11 Which is the name of the space telescope that was launched on April 24, 1990, and began taking pictures of the universe?

a. Voyager
c. Calypso
b. Hubble
d. The Eye

CHECK YOUR ANSWERS ON PAGES 172–173.

Powers of Nature

1 According to popular legend, how was the Great Chicago Fire started?

a. A cow kicked over a lantern.
b. Lightning hit a lumberyard.
c. A coal mine exploded.
d. A backyard barbecue got seriously out of control.

2 Which technology was first used to track weather during World War II?

a. weather balloon
b. radar
c. thermometer
d. anemometer

3 Which type of natural disaster took place in Fukushima, Japan, in 2011?

a. a gravity wave
b. a hurricane
c. an earthquake
d. a zombie outbreak

4 Which city was buried when Mount Vesuvius in Italy erupted in A.D. 79?

a. Venice
b. Pompeii
c. New York
d. Hogsmeade

5 In March 1942, the most rain ever recorded in one month fell in Maui, Hawaii. How much of the wet stuff did they get?

a. 1 foot (30 cm)
b. 9 feet (3 m)
c. 15 feet (4.5 m)
d. 30 feet (9 m)

6 In the 1940s, which of these places was a new spot for surfers looking to catch some waves in the winter?

a. Lake Michigan
b. Mississippi River
c. Black Sea
d. Nile River

7 In 2010, the world's largest known hailstone was measured to be the size of a _____.

a. tomato
b. softball
c. volleyball
d. watermelon

SURFER

8 A rare fire rainbow was spotted in Scotland in July 2012, lasting only _____ before it disappeared.

a. 5 seconds
b. 20 seconds
c. 5 minutes
d. 20 minutes

9 Which of the following was NOT the name of a major hurricane to hit the United States?

a. Katrina
b. Wallis
c. Ike
d. Rita

FIRE RAINBOW

10 **True or false?** Iraq's 2009 sandstorm lasted almost two days.

11 Water spouts sometimes pick up animals and then "rain" them down. Animals that have fallen from the sky have included fish, worms, and _____.

a. poodles
b. eagles
c. frogs
d. unicorns

WATER SPOUT

CHECK YOUR ANSWERS ON PAGES 172–173.

MAP MANIA!

STILL STANDING

1 BIG BEN

The name "Big Ben" today often refers to the clock, tower, and bell. Which was the original Big Ben?
a. The Great Bell
b. The Great Clock
c. Elizabeth Tower
d. The King of England's friend, Ben.

2 EIFFEL TOWER

True or false? When it was built in 1889, the Eiffel Tower was the tallest building in the world.

3 THE SPHINX

Why is the Sphinx missing its nose?
a. It was eroded by sandstorms.
b. It was destroyed by a person.
c. It was built without a nose.
d. It sneezed a little too hard.

4 LEANING TOWER OF PISA

True or false? The Leaning Tower of Pisa started leaning while it was being built.

NORTH AMERICA

BLARNEY, IRELAND

ATLANTIC OCEAN

PACIFIC OCEAN

SOUTH AMERICA

These famous structures have been around for quite a while! Test your knowledge about each cool construction and then match each one to its location.

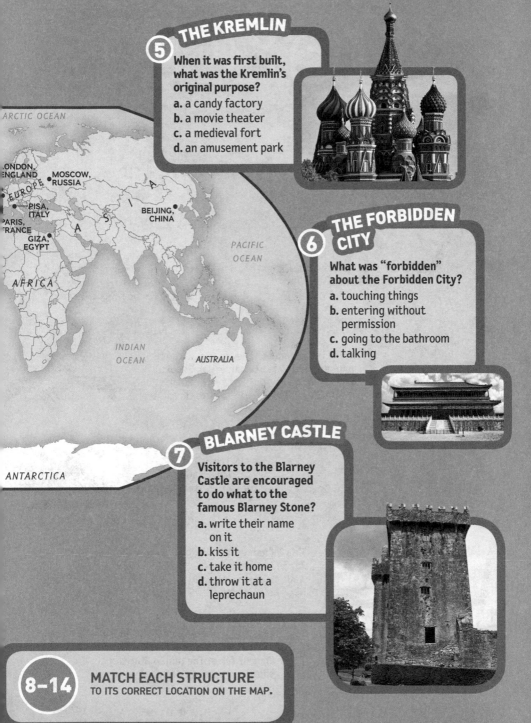

THE KREMLIN

5 When it was first built, what was the Kremlin's original purpose?

a. a candy factory
b. a movie theater
c. a medieval fort
d. an amusement park

ARCTIC OCEAN

LONDON, ENGLAND
MOSCOW, RUSSIA
EUROPE
PISA, ITALY
PARIS, FRANCE
GIZA, EGYPT
AFRICA
A S I A
BEIJING, CHINA
PACIFIC OCEAN
INDIAN OCEAN
AUSTRALIA
ANTARCTICA

THE FORBIDDEN CITY

6 What was "forbidden" about the Forbidden City?

a. touching things
b. entering without permission
c. going to the bathroom
d. talking

BLARNEY CASTLE

7 Visitors to the Blarney Castle are encouraged to do what to the famous Blarney Stone?

a. write their name on it
b. kiss it
c. take it home
d. throw it at a leprechaun

8–14 **MATCH EACH STRUCTURE** TO ITS CORRECT LOCATION ON THE MAP.

Trends for the 2000s

1 Which was the name of the robotic hamster that became a fad in 2009?

a. Alvin
b. Zhu Zhu
c. Pikachu
d. John Smith

2 Which J. K. Rowling book is the fastest-selling book in history?

a. *Harry Potter and the Sorcerer's Stone*
b. *Harry Potter and the Goblet of Fire*
c. *Harry Potter and the Deathly Hallows*
d. *Harry Potter and the Half-Blood Prince*

3 Which is the name of the number puzzle that became popular in the 2000s?

a. karaoke
b. Sudoku
c. Rubik's Cube
d. tic-tac-toe

SPACE SHUTTLE
ATLANTIS

4 **True or false?** Barack Obama was elected as the first African American President of the United States in 2008.

5 This TV movie starring Zac Efron and Vanessa Anne Hudgens was a huge hit in 2006.

a. *Zenon: The Zequel*
b. *High School Musical*
c. *Stepsister From Planet Weird*
d. *Angels in the Infield*

6 **True or false?** The United States space shuttle program ended in 2011.

Atlantis

7 What is the name of the currency that 17 countries in Europe use, which first began circulating in the 2000s?

a. the dollar
b. the exchanger
c. the euro
d. the continental

8 Kenny George, a college basketball player during the 2000s, had feet that were bigger than the largest athletic shoe size commonly made. What size shoe did George wear?

a. 19
b. 23
c. 25
d. 30

9 True or false? Toyota's hybrid car, the Prius, first went on sale in 2000.

10 In the 2000s, which television network had hits that included *Chowder*, *Samurai Jack*, and *Foster's Home for Imaginary Friends*?

a. Cartoon Network
b. Boomerang
c. Nickelodeon
d. Disney XD

11 What is the name, first used in 2003, for a group of people who use the Internet to organize a gathering, do something together, and then leave?

a. Quick Flock
b. Flash Mob
c. Jiffy Gather
d. Hasty Horde

12 Who is the artist who made the 2012 hit "Gangnam Style" song and dance?

a. Psy
b. Justin Bieber
c. Beyoncé
d. Taylor Swift

CHECK YOUR ANSWERS ON PAGES 172–173.

American Pioneers

1. PIONEERS TRAVELING IN THE MID-1800S ALONG THE OREGON TRAIL, A ROUTE FROM THE EASTERN UNITED STATES TO THE NORTHWESTERN TERRITORIES, MOSTLY USED RAGS WHEN "NATURE CALLED."

2. MANY PIONEERS LEFT THE EASTERN UNITED STATES AND TRAVELED WEST IN SEARCH OF GOLD.

3. THE LEWIS AND CLARK EXPEDITION, A TRIP ORGANIZED BY PRESIDENT THOMAS JEFFERSON TO EXPLORE THE WESTERN TERRITORY OF THE UNITED STATES, INCLUDED A DOG ON THE TRIP.

4. THE MOST COMMON INJURY FOR PIONEERS TRAVELING ALONG THE OREGON TRAIL WAS GETTING RUN OVER BY WAGONS.

5. A PIONEER WAGON COST ABOUT $1,000.

6. A FAMILY OF FOUR TRAVELING DURING THE 1800S USED ABOUT 1,000 POUNDS (453.5 KG) OF FOOD ON THE JOURNEY ALONG THE OREGON TRAIL.

7. PEOPLE GREASED WAGON AXLES WITH BUTTER.

8. IF YOU WERE TO TRAVEL WEST IN THE 1800S, YOU MIGHT FIND STOVES, TRUNKS, AND WAGONS THAT PIONEERS LEFT ALONG THE WAY.

9. SOME PIONEERS TOOK ALONG CHOCOLATE FOR A SPECIAL TREAT.

10. A LARGE PIONEER WAGON WAS ABOUT THE SAME LENGTH AS A MODERN MINIVAN.

11. RIDERS FOR THE OLD MAIL SERVICE CALLED THE PONY EXPRESS SWITCHED HORSES AT EVERY STATION TO KEEP UP A GOOD SPEED.

12. MOST OF THE PIONEERS IN THE 1800S WERE BUSINESSPEOPLE.

13. PIONEERS TRAVELING IN THE WILDERNESS OFTEN USED BUFFALO DUNG AS FUEL FOR FIRES.

14. NATIVE AMERICANS WERE ALWAYS HOSTILE AND THREATENING TO PIONEERS.

15. MOST WAGONS IN THE 1800S WERE PULLED BY HORSES.

16 CHILDREN OF PIONEER FAMILIES USUALLY HAD THEIR OWN BEDROOMS.

17 PIONEERS IN THE 1800S INVENTED THE SPORT OF BASEBALL.

18 PIONEERS OFTEN WROTE MESSAGES ON ANIMAL SKULLS AND LEFT THEM IN "PRAIRIE POST OFFICES" FOR OTHER TRAVELERS TO READ.

19 WHEN PIONEERS DIED DURING THEIR JOURNEY, THEY WERE OFTEN BURIED IN THE MIDDLE OF THE ROAD.

20 LEWIS AND CLARK RECEIVED HELP FROM NATIVE AMERICANS WHILE THEY WERE TRAVELING.

21 SOME PIONEERS CARRIED ONLY AN AX AND A RIFLE AS SUPPLIES—NOTHING ELSE.

22 PIONEERS USED DEER AND BEAR FAT TO MAKE CANDLES IN THE 1800S.

23 EXPLORER MERIWETHER LEWIS WAS SHOT IN THE REAR DURING HIS TRIP BECAUSE SOMEONE THOUGHT HE WAS AN ELK.

24 A JOURNEY ON THE OREGON TRAIL FROM CALIFORNIA TO OREGON COULD BE COMPLETED IN THREE MONTHS.

25 PIONEERS COLLECTED BONES THEY FOUND AS SOUVENIRS.

26 TYPICAL LOG CABINS IN THE 1800S WERE USUALLY ONLY ABOUT 4 FEET (1.2 M) HIGH.

27 A TYPICAL WAGON TRAIN IN THE 1800S TRAVELED ABOUT 200 MILES (321.8 KM) A DAY.

28 MANY PIONEER CHILDREN WENT TO SCHOOL ONLY FROM OCTOBER TO MAY.

29 PIONEERS SOMETIMES EXTRACTED SALT FROM SALT FIELDS THEY FOUND AS THEY TRAVELED.

30 TOURISTS CAN NOW TAKE WAGON TRAIN TRIPS ALONG PARTS OF THE ORIGINAL OREGON TRAIL ROUTE.

Middle Ages Mayhem

1 True or false? Country people in England during the Middle Ages slept with their farm animals in the house.

2 Jousting knights on horseback would charge toward each other at incredible speed. How fast did they go?

a. 15 miles an hour (24 km/h)
b. 33 miles an hour (53 km/h)
c. 60 miles an hour (96.5 km/h)
d. 150 miles an hour (241 km/h)

3 Which of these items was NOT invented during the Middle Ages?

a. eyeglasses
b. the magnetic compass
c. the lie detector
d. the thermometer

4 What did some people believe would cure warts?

a. spiderwebs
b. frog saliva
c. bubble gum
d. dragon scales

5 In the Middle Ages, what did women in Florence, Italy, do as a fashion statement?

a. dye their hair purple
b. wear braces on their teeth
c. shave off their eyebrows
d. grow long beards

6 The famous scientist Galileo discovered the moons of which planet during the Middle Ages?

a. Pluto
b. Jupiter
c. Uranus
d. Mercury

7 Castles had indoor bathrooms called privies or garderobes. What happened to the waste material?

a. It was flushed into a sewer.
b. It was dumped into the moat or on the ground.
c. It was dried and burned for fuel.
d. It was catapulted to another town.

8 True or False? Under medieval law, animals could be tried and sentenced for crimes such as stealing.

9 Which board game was first introduced to Europe in the Middle Ages by people from the Middle East?

a. Monopoly
b. dominoes
c. Dungeons & Dragons
d. chess

10 During the Middle Ages, a barber often had two other jobs. Which were they?

a. teacher and acrobat
b. chef and waiter
c. tax collector and sheriff
d. surgeon and dentist

GAME SHOW

ULTIMATE HISTORY CHALLENGE

1 Which is the name of this hairdo that was popular in the 1960s?

a. rattrap   **b.** anthill

c. beehive   **d.** bird nest

2 The Indian Ocean tsunami of 2004 was one of the strongest and deadliest in history. How far did this megawave travel?

a. 200 miles (321 km)

b. 999 miles (1,607 km)

c. 3,000 miles (5,000 km)

d. 10,000 miles (16,093 km)

3 In the 1990s, one fad was T-shirts that changed color due to _____.

a. noise

b. body heat

c. mood

d. body odor

4 The term "piggy bank" started in the Middle Ages as "pygg pots," which were pots for storing money. What type of material was pygg?

a. clay   **b.** steel

c. wood   **d.** plastic

5 **TRUE OR FALSE?** When Amazon.com first started in 1995, the owner began by shipping books out of his garage.

6 The tallest building in the world is the Burj Khalifa. Where is it located?

a. Dubai

b. Tokyo

c. Moscow

d. Gotham City

7 If someone in the 1990s said, "You are all that and a bag of chips!" what were they really saying?

a. "I'm hungry for a sandwich!"

b. "You should work at a grocery store!"

c. "You look like you eat a lot!"

d. "You're the best and then some!"

8 During a medieval knighting ceremony, the king or other official tapped the would-be knight with the flat of the hand or broad side of the sword and said, "I _____ thee sir knight."
a. dub
b. rub-a-dub-dub
c. nickname
d. bonk

9 In the Middle Ages, how did people believe they could catch a disease?
a. by being bitten by a horse
b. by smelling a foul or bad odor
c. by washing their hands
d. by using bad language

10 TRUE OR FALSE? Amusement parks got their start in Europe in the Middle Ages.

11 TRUE OR FALSE? At first, only college students could join Facebook.

12 In 1992, Euro Disney opened in which European city?
a. London
b. Paris
c. Berlin
d. Madrid

13 Which of the following games did pioneer children in the 1800s NOT play?
a. dominoes
b. tiddlywinks
c. charades
d. crazy eights

14 TRUE OR FALSE? King Richard of England once gave a feast for 10,000 people.

15 ULTIMATE BRAIN BUSTER

CAN YOU NAME THIS PONY EXPRESS RIDER WHO LATER TRAVELED AND PERFORMED TRICK SHOTS WITH HIS PISTOLS? HINT: IF YOU THINK IT'S "BISON BART," YOU'RE CLOSE.

Eat My Words!

1 Roald Dahl wrote a book about a boy and a giant piece of which fruit?

a. peach
b. plum
c. pineapple
d. pear

2 *Bunnicula* is a story about a bunny that does what?

a. turns into a bat
b. bites vegetables and drains them of their juices
c. grows garlic to fight vampires
d. lives on a farm in Transylvania

CANDY HEARTS

3 In the nursery rhyme "Little Jack Horner," what was Jack eating?

a. Christmas pie
b. Thanksgiving turkey
c. candy hearts
d. chocolate eggs

4 In what folktale does a hungry stranger trick a villager into helping him make a delicious meal?

a. "Yummy Casserole"
b. "Stone Soup"
c. "Tricky Pizza"
d. "Delish Dish"

5 Shel Silverstein's poem "Hungry Mungry" is about a boy who eats which of the following?

a. a shank of lamb
b. four chocolate shakes
c. the universe
d. all of the above

6 True or false? The strange food weather in the book *Cloudy With a Chance of Meatballs* takes place in the village of YumYumville.

7 **True or false?** In the movie *Ratatouille*, Remy the rat creates a delicious vegetable stew.

8 Which is the name of a book by Judy Bloom about a boy who makes a disgusting drink in order to get freckles?

a. *Freckle Shake*
b. *Freckle Potion*
c. *Freckle Fountain*
d. *Freckle Juice*

9 Hans Christian Andersen wrote a famous fairy tale about a girl who can feel which food under her mattress?

a. a soybean
b. a banana
c. a pork chop
d. a pea

10 In the song "On Top of Spaghetti," what was lost when somebody sneezed?

a. noodles
b. marshmallows
c. a meatball
d. a sense of humor

NARNIA
THE LION, THE WITCH AND THE WARDROBE
BASED ON THE ORIGINAL BOOK BY
C. S. Lewis
Illustrated by Tudor Humphries

11 **True or false?** In the book *The Chronicles of Narnia: The Lion, the Witch and the Wardrobe*, the White Witch gives Edmund a slice of coconut cake at their first meeting.

Mind Your Manners

1 In Chile, which is the preferred method for eating french fries?

a. eating them with a knife and fork
b. eating them from a paper cone
c. eating them with lots of ketchup
d. eating them inside sandwiches and burgers

2 In traditional Korean dining, where would guests sit?

a. on the floor
b. at a round table
c. on the sidewalk
d. outdoors

3 True or false? In Japan, it is considered rude to stand your chopsticks up in your rice bowl.

4 The Continental style of dining favored by Europeans means what?

a. Plates are in the different shapes of continents.
b. A fork is held in your left hand and a knife in your right.
c. All meals are eaten outdoors.
d. Dining guests are expected to name all continents before getting dessert.

5 What does the book *Emily Post's Table Manners for Kids* advise about texting when dining?

a. It is perfectly acceptable.
b. It is acceptable if the host is also texting.
c. It is acceptable to text once dessert is served.
d. It is never acceptable to text during a meal.

6 What do Bedouins in the Middle East do to signal that they do not want more coffee?

a. put a chair on the table
b. shake a cup
c. shout, "Enough!"
d. wink three times

7 Which food did early Greeks give guests as a symbol of hospitality?

a. olives
b. bananas
c. Greek salad
d. salt

8 If a German host calls out "Guten Appetit!" before you eat, what is the host saying to you?

a. "May your gut be filled with good food."
b. "German food is yummy."
c. "Enjoy your meal!"
d. "Rub-a-dub-dub, here comes the grub!"

9 True or false? Loudly slurping soup in Japan is an offense that carries a hefty fine.

10 Which custom is common to many parts of Asia, Africa, and the Middle East but not to Europe and the United States?

a. singing at the table
b. eating with your hands
c. not speaking at the table
d. eating dessert first

11 In South India, you should never touch your plate with what?

a. your fork
b. your neighbor's elbow
c. a shoe
d. your left hand

Snacks From the Sea

1 **True or false?** The amount of wild fish and shellfish caught from the ocean each year is about three times the total weight of every person in the United States.

3 **What is another name for the Chilean sea bass, a popular fish served in many seafood restaurants?**

a. Patagonian toothfish
b. slippery codswallop
c. joker fish
d. SpongeBob BigBass

5 **True or false?** Roughly half of all seafood is raised and farmed by humans.

2 **What is the name of a tasty fish found in southeast Asia that can move short distances over land?**

a. U-Haul fish
c. walking catfish
b. lungfish
d. blue jumper

4 **A cousin to the grouper that is also popular for dinner is called _____ in South Carolina, U.S.A.**

a. cousin flipper
b. wreckfish
c. Sam
d. blue whale

6 **How is the tambaqui different from its flesh-eating cousin, the piranha?**

a. It only eats the flesh of hippos.
b. It is vegetarian.
c. It has legs.
d. It has twice as many teeth.

7 Black squid ink is a popular ingredient in some pasta dishes. Why do squid squirt ink?

a. to confuse predators
b. to attract a mate
c. to use in letter writing
d. to show off

8 What live seafood can be bought at a vending machine in China?

a. octopus   b. sardines
c. slithering eels d. hairy crabs

9 True or false? A bluefin tuna weighing 754 pounds (342 kg) sold at auction in Tokyo for $420,000.

10 On *The Simpsons* television show, what was the name of Homer Simpson's pet lobster?

a. Claws   b. Sir Grab-A-Lot
c. Pinchy   d. Bart

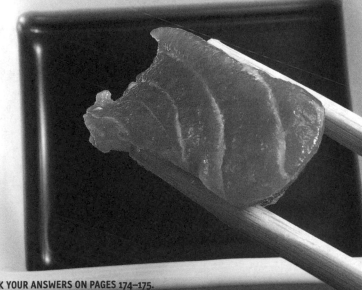

MAP MANIA!
Global Grub

① TURKEY

True or false? The shish kebab may have originated with medieval Turkish soldiers who used their swords to grill meat over open fires.

NORTH AMERICA

C

E

PACIFIC OCEAN

ATLANTIC OCEAN

SOUTH AMERICA

② ICELAND

In addition to smoking salmon, some people in Iceland catch this fish and let it rot before eating it.

a. halibut
b. catfish
c. goldfish
d. shark

③ MEXICO

On the Day of the Dead in Mexico, people bake a sweet bread called *pan de muerto*. What does *pan de muerto* mean?

a. bone bread
b. snacker crackers
c. bread of the dead
d. pan of skeleton

How much do you know about grub around the globe? Test your knowledge of food traditions from many cultures and then match each yummy treat to the country where it came from on the map.

4 GERMANY

Which surprising ingredient can often be found in Germany's traditional cookie *pfeffernüsse*? Hint: You might find it near the salt.

a. eye of newt
b. pepper
c. mango
d. candy canes

ARCTIC OCEAN

EUROPE

B

D

ASIA

AFRICA

A

PACIFIC OCEAN

INDIAN OCEAN

F

5 AUSTRALIA

Pavlova, a popular meringue dessert topped with fruit, was created to honor which famous person after a visit to Australia?

a. Russian ballerina Anna Pavlova
b. Jamaican bobsled champion Deon Pavlova
c. British teen pop star Pavlova Spears
d. Polish president Pyotr Pavlova

ANTARCTICA

6 SOUTH AFRICA

True or false? Bunny chow is a traditional South African dish of curried rabbit served in a bread bowl.

7-12 RED MARKERS SHOW

WHERE EACH OF THESE TASTY MORSELS CAN BE FOUND. MATCH EACH FOOD TO ITS COUNTRY OF ORIGIN ON THE MAP.

CHECK YOUR ANSWERS ON PAGES 174–175.

TRUEorFALSE?

Extreme Eats

1 A 1,000-POUND (453-KG) BUTTER SCULPTURE ON DISPLAY AT A FAIR WAS LATER USED TO PROVIDE ELECTRICITY ON A FARM FOR THREE DAYS.

2 THE LATIN NAME FOR COCOA IS *THEOBROMA*, WHICH LITERALLY MEANS "SWEET DARKNESS."

3 MORE THAN 700 PEOPLE IN DALLAS, TEXAS, U.S.A., DRESSED AS CLOWNS AND HAD A CREAM PIE FIGHT TO RAISE MONEY FOR CHARITIES.

4 DURIAN FRUIT IS SO SMELLY IT IS NOT ALLOWED ON PUBLIC TRANSPORTATION IN SOUTHEAST ASIA.

5 A WOMAN IN SUSSEX, ENGLAND, U.K., ATE 7,175 PEAS IN 60 MINUTES.

6 MORE THAN 40,000 PEOPLE POUR INTO THE STREETS AND HURL CHEESE AT EACH OTHER DURING SPAIN'S LA TOMATINA FESTIVAL.

7 THE WORLD RECORD FOR THE NUMBER OF EARTHWORMS EATEN IN 30 SECONDS IS 59.

8 IN INDONESIA, SNAKE MEAT IS CONSIDERED TABOO AND IS NEVER EATEN.

9 EDIBLE LEAFCUTTER ANTS ARE BEING PROMOTED AS A HIGH-PROTEIN ALTERNATIVE TO BEEF AND PORK.

10 A GROUP CALLED "CANSTRUCTION" SPONSORS DESIGN COMPETITIONS WHERE PARTICIPANTS BUILD STRUCTURES MADE ENTIRELY OF CANNED GOODS.

11 THE WINNER OF AN EATING CONTEST IN CALIFORNIA, U.S.A., ATE 55 DUMPLINGS IN 10 MINUTES.

12 AN ITALIAN CHEESE MADE OF SHEEP'S MILK IS SOFTENED THROUGH THE INTRODUCTION OF MAGGOTS.

13 THE UNITED KINGDOM'S HELEN JUCKES HOLDS THE RECORD FOR THE FASTEST MARATHON TIME FOR A FEMALE DRESSED AS A STALK OF BROCCOLI.

14 THE WORLD'S LARGEST PIZZA DELIVERY HAPPENED WITH 30,000 PIZZAS SENT FROM ILLINOIS, U.S.A., TO THE ARMED FORCES IN AFGHANISTAN.

A POTATO CHIP FLAVORED LIKE ROAST OX CAN BE FOUND IN PERU.

16 THE POMELO IS A CITRUS FRUIT OFTEN GIVEN AS A GIFT DURING MEXICO'S DAY OF THE DEAD CELEBRATION.

7 THE DANDELION, CONSIDERED A WEED BY GARDENERS, IS ALSO EATEN AS A SALAD GREEN.

18 A QUAHOG IS ANOTHER NAME FOR A CUPCAKE.

19 IN FINLAND, YOU CAN DINE IN A CAVE RESTAURANT 262 FEET (80 M) UNDERGROUND.

20 YOU CAN BE SERVED BY ROBOTS IN A HONG KONG RESTAURANT CALLED ROBOT KITCHEN.

21 YOU CANNOT SQUEEZE JUICE FROM A CACTUS.

22 A SAN FRANCISCO ENGINEER HAS CREATED A LIQUID THAT HE CLAIMS WILL REPLACE FOOD IN THE FUTURE.

23 A TYPE OF CHILI PEPPER GROWN IN INDIA IS THREE THOUSAND TO FOUR THOUSAND TIMES HOTTER THAN A JALAPEÑO.

24 VULTURES CAN DINE ON TASTY ROADKILL AT A SPECIAL VULTURE RESTAURANT IN TURKEY.

25 STRAW IS THE PRIMARY INGREDIENT IN THE CHINESE DELICACY BIRD'S NEST SOUP.

26 IN SWEDEN, BEEF TONGUE ICE CREAM IS A POPULAR FLAVOR.

27 IN 1919, A TANK FILLED WITH MORE THAN 2 MILLION GALLONS (7.5 MILLION L) OF MOLASSES EXPLODED AND FLOODED STREETS IN BOSTON, MASSACHUSETTS, U.S.A.

28 TO MAKE MILK LOOK FRESHLY POURED IN ADVERTISEMENTS, PUDDING IS ADDED TO MAKE FROTHY BUBBLES.

29 A BRITISH CANDY MAKER MADE A GOLD-COVERED CHOCOLATE CANDY BAR.

0 IN A RESTAURANT IN SYDNEY, AUSTRALIA, YOU CAN ORDER A ROO PIZZA THAT INCLUDES STRIPS OF MARINATED CROCODILE.

CHECK YOUR ANSWERS ON PAGES 174–175.

Grow Your Groceries

1 How many pounds of tomatoes does the average American eat each year?

a. 2 pounds (.9 kg)
b. 22 pounds (10 kg)
c. 40 pounds (18 kg)
d. 180 pounds (82 kg)

2 True or false? Raspberries and blueberries have long been used as dyes to color cotton and wool.

3 About how many squirts of milk from a cow does it take to make a gallon of milk?

a. 15
b. 79
c. 150
d. 350

4 How many honeybees does it take to make one tablespoon of honey?

a. 1
b. 12
c. 50
d. 1,500

5 How many gallons of water are needed to produce one bushel of corn?

a. 12
b. 50
c. 500
d. 4,000

6 A Roman emperor's son loved which vegetable so much that he refused to eat anything else for an entire month?

a. broccoli
b. string beans
c. carrots
d. beets

7 Eggplants are related to which food?

a. beets
b. tomatoes
c. potatoes
d. plums

8 Which U.S. state grows the most grapes?

a. Montana
b. Florida
c. California
d. Hawaii

9 Which of the following has been used to treat headaches, toothaches, animal bites, and the plague?

a. yams
b. applesauce
c. garlic
d. spinach

10 Which food is believed to be the first crop grown for food?

a. apples
b. figs
c. broccoli
d. popcorn

11 **True or false?** Squash got its name from a cooking method in which the gourd was squashed before baking.

12 The strawberry is a member of which plant family?

a. cherry
b. rose
c. pumpkin
d. Venus flytrap

CHECK YOUR ANSWERS ON PAGES 174–175.

Street Food

KOSHARI

1 Egypt's national dish, *koshari*, is a spicy stew filled with rice, lentils, garlic, and chickpeas and topped with what?
a. raw eggs
b. crispy fried onions
c. glitter
d. lemon peel

2 Where are you most likely to find street vendors selling barbecued stingrays?
a. at a very weird water park
b. Denmark
c. Malaysia
d. the lost food court of Atlantis

BARBECUED STINGRAY

3 What is the name of a common fried dough treat found at amusement parks in the United States?
a. puffed sugar pies
b. fry puppies
c. fun dough
d. funnel cake

4 Which of the following rodents is a popular grilled food in Peru?
a. mole rat
b. guinea pig
c. porcupine
d. gerbil

5 Which skewered treat is sold in the Philippines?
a. chicken intestines
b. earthworms
c. candied string beans
d. barbecued beef jerky

6 What hearty lunch soup can you buy from vendors in Shanghai?
a. alphabet soup with carrots
b. ostrich and onions
c. split pea with artichoke
d. duck blood and glass noodle

7 Which of these foods is a common sweet treat in Malaysia?
a. jackfruit
b. alligator snouts
c. goose in cherry soup
d. lemon puffs

8 True or false? Deep-fried spiders are a crunchy snack sold in Cambodia.

TARANTULA

9 What chocolate-covered treat was served at a street festival in New York? Hint: It was also green.
a. pickle
b. fish eye
c. Italian sausage
d. frog leg

10 True or false? Some food trucks in Alaska, U.S.A., sell reindeer hot dogs.

11 A bouquet of grasshoppers in China's street food scene provides a healthy boost of what?
a. vitamin C
b. protein
c. sugar
d. carbohydrates

GRASSHOPPERS

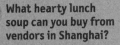

CHECK YOUR ANSWERS ON PAGES 174–175.

Sweet Treats

1 The world's first desserts were probably eaten in ____.

a. U.S.A.
b. India
c. France
d. Russia

2 True or false? Bees in France began producing blue and green honey when they fed on waste from a nearby M&M candy factory.

3 Which of the following is *not* a Bertie Bott's jellybean flavor from the *Harry Potter* series?

a. centipede
b. paper
c. toenails
d. whistle spit

4 At Greek weddings it is customary to serve an odd number of pieces of this candy to wedding guests.

a. Easter eggs
b. candy canes
c. candy-coated almonds
d. Hershey's kisses

5 According to ice-cream maker Baskin-Robbins, if you like chocolate chip ice cream, you are probably a ____ person.

a. cautious
b. confident
c. generous
d. dramatic

6 Cotton candy made its debut at the 1904 World's Fair. What was its original name?

a. sticky stucco
b. fairy floss
c. pink tornado
d. spun fun

7 True or false? The owners of Krispy Kreme doughnuts cut a hole in the side of their bakery so they could sell to people on the sidewalk.

8 How much water does it take to make one pound (.5 kg) of dark chocolate?

a. 1 gallon (4 L)
b. 27 gallons (102 L)
c. 542 gallons (2,052 L)
d. 3,170 gallons (12,000 L)

9 True or false? White chocolate does not contain any chocolate.

10 One British candy maker claims to have made a chocolate bar that doesn't do what?

a. melt
b. taste good
c. look like chocolate
d. hold a shape

11 Which ingredient is not included in traditional fudge?

a. butter
b. chocolate
c. sugar
d. milk

ECK YOUR ANSWERS ON PAGES 174–175.

GAME SHOW

ULTIMATE FOOD CHALLENGE

1 When bees visit flowers, what do they eat and later turn into honey?
a. nectar
b. leaf
c. stem
d. root

2 In which state could you find a giant statue of a buttered, baked potato in front of a museum?
a. Rhode Island
b. Idaho
c. Florida
d. Hawaii

3 What does the video game character Pac-Man eat?
a. candy corn
b. barbecued bananas
c. mushroom magnets
d. power pellets

4 Which type of restaurant is most associated with Brazil?
a. sushi bar
b. pizza place
c. noodle shop
d. steak house

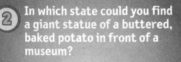

5 NASA astronaut Don Pettit wrote about growing vegetables on the International Space Station. What was the name of his blog?
a. Broccoli Rocket
b. Mean Green Space Beans
c. Diary of a Space Zucchini
d. Try to Beet Me to Mars

6 A hawk that eats a frog that eats a grasshopper that eats grass is an example of what?
a. bad manners
b. food chain
c. ecosystem
d. nature gone wild

7 TRUE OR FALSE?
A long time ago, people would expose fruits and vegetables to the sun and wind in order to preserve them.

8 In Japan, you can buy natto, a slimy dish of fermented _____.

a. horsehair
b. soybeans
c. eel
d. asparagus

9 Early Egyptian craftspeople created a multi-use tool with a bowl shape at one end and what at the other end?

a. a hook to extract snails from their shells
b. a fork with six tines
c. scissors for cutting hair
d. a sword

10 # TRUE OR FALSE?

The Central Andean Indians in Peru were not successful at growing crops at high elevations.

11 What is cooked in an outdoor pit at the traditional Hawaiian feast known as the luau?

a. pig
b. fish
c. spinach
d. pumpkin soup

12 _____ was so important to the medieval diet, there were laws about baking and selling it.

a. bread
b. cabbage
c. meat
d. pizza

13 While some mushrooms are edible, a beautiful mushroom known as the _____ is highly poisonous!

a. skull and crossbones
b. death cap
c. mush of death
d. goner 'shroom

14 # TRUE OR FALSE?

A key ingredient in shoofly pie is a common housefly.

15 **ULTIMATE BRAIN BUSTER** SHAVING CREAM, GLUE, AND EXPLOSIVES ARE JUST A FEW OF THE PRODUCTS MADE FROM WHICH FOOD?

a. eggs
b. carrots
c. peanuts
d. ice pops

Think Fast!

CLUB-WINGED MANAKIN

1 Zdeno Chara of the Boston Bruins ice hockey team set a National Hockey League record for the fastest slap shot. How fast was it?

a. 4 miles an hour (6 km/h)
b. 55 miles an hour (88 km/h)
c. 108 miles an hour (174 km/h)
d. 697 miles an hour (1,122 km/h)

2 How fast did professional speedster Usain Bolt run the 100-meter dash at the 2012 London Olympics?

a. 2.3 seconds
b. 9.63 seconds
c. 1 minute 4 seconds
d. 10 minutes 17 seconds

BLACK MAMBA

3 If you wanted to outrun the black mamba, the fastest snake in the world, how fast would you need to scoot?

a. only about 5 miles an hour (8 km/h)
b. at least 15 miles an hour (24 km/h)
c. at least 30 miles an hour (48 km/h)
d. at least 60 miles an hour (97 km/h)

4 Which car can reach speeds of 267 miles an hour (430 km/h)?

a. Chevrolet Corvette
b. Alfa Romeo
c. Volkswagen Beetle
d.  Bugatti Veyron Super Spo

5 China's CRH308A is the fastest way to travel on land legally. What is the CRH380A?

a. a group of cars chained together
b. a tour bus for a rock-and-roll band
c. a train
d. a horse that drank a lot of coffee

6 The male club-winged manakin can flap its wings the fastest of any bird. Why this need for speed?

a. to attract a mate
b. to fly into space
c. to fan away pests
d. to make humming-birds feel like losers

7 Which animal can run more than 40 miles an hour (64 km/h), making it the world's fastest running bird?

a. an ostrich
b. a penguin
c. a roadrunner
d. a kiwi

8 **True or false?** The fastest any human has ever traveled is 24,791 miles an hour (39,897 km/h).

9 The fastest piloted airplane can travel more than 2,000 miles an hour (3,218 km/h). What is its name?

a. the Blackberry
b. the Black Panther
c. the Blackbird
d. the Holy Cow That's Fast!

GENTOO PENGUIN

10 Which bird of prey can dive at speeds that are faster than the average race car can drive?

a. a chicken
b. a peregrine falcon
c. a turkey vulture
d. a duck

11 Where is the world's fastest roller coaster?

a. Six Flags, Jackson, New Jersey, U.S.A.
b. Cedar Point, Sandusky, Ohio, U.S.A.
c. Fuji-Q Highland, Yamanashi, Japan
d. Ferrari World, Abu Dhabi, U.A.E.

ROLLER COASTER

CHECK YOUR ANSWERS ON PAGES 175–176.

TRUE or FALSE?

Freaky Figures

1 IT IS IMPOSSIBLE FOR A PERSON TO SPIT A WATERMELON SEED FARTHER THAN 50 FEET (15 M).

2 A MAN FROM TEXAS, U.S.A., SPENT 45 MINUTES IN A BATHTUB WITH 87 VENOMOUS RATTLESNAKES.

3 THE WORLD RECORD FOR SKIPPING STONES ACROSS WATER IS 40 SKIPS.

4 A BROWN RECLUSE SPIDER CAN HAVE MORE THAN 1,000 SPIDERLINGS A YEAR.

5 CHOCOLATE CAN BE MADE INTO A BAR THAT WEIGHS AS MUCH AS AN ELEPHANT.

6 THE LARGEST FRESHWATER FISH EVER CAUGHT WAS A CATFISH IN THAILAND THAT WEIGHED 646 POUNDS (293 KG).

7 THE YOUNGEST PROFESSIONAL DRUMMER RECORDED HIS FIRST CD WHEN HE WAS 20 MONTHS OLD.

8 A MAN IN INDIA GREW HIS MOUSTACHE 14 FEET (4 M) LONG IN ONLY FIVE YEARS.

9 TWO FORMER MARINES RODE THEIR BICYCLES UNDERWATER FOR 100 MILES (161 KM).

10 IT'S POSSIBLE FOR HAIR TO GROW MORE THAN THREE TIMES THE LENGTH OF AN AVERAGE ADULT'S BODY.

11 A 7-YEAR-OLD BOY IN UKRAINE ONCE DID 4,000 PUSH-UPS IN A ROW.

12 THE WORLD RECORD FOR THE LONGEST BURP IS 18.1 MINUTES.

13 IT'S IMPOSSIBLE TO DO A BREAK-DANCING HEAD SPIN FOR MORE THAN FIVE MINUTES.

14 A 10-YEAR-OLD GIRL FROM NEW JERSEY, U.S.A., CAN SQUAT POWER-LIFT 226 POUNDS (102.5 KG).

15 HENS CAN LAY ABOUT 265 EGGS A YEAR.

16 TO RAISE MONEY FOR CHARITY, OVER 800 PEOPLE IN ENGLAND GATHERED TOGETHER DRESSED AS BATMAN.

17 A PERSON'S SCREAM IS LOUDER THAN AN AMBULANCE SIREN.

18 A MAN ONCE CLIMBED 16 MILES (25.7 KM) UP MOUNT FUJI ON A POGO STICK.

19 AT 50 YEARS OLD, TAMAE WATANABE BECAME THE OLDEST WOMAN TO CLIMB MOUNT EVEREST.

20 THE MOST LIVING CREATURES EVER CAST IN A MOVIE WERE THE 22 MILLION BEES THAT APPEARED IN *THE SWARM*.

21 A PERSON ONCE WATCHED MOVIES CONTINUOUSLY FOR OVER FIVE DAYS.

22 IF YOU WRITE DOWN THE NAMES OF ALL THE CARDS IN A DECK EXCEPT THE JOKER AND COUNT ALL THE LETTERS, THE TOTAL IS 52—THE SAME AS THE NUMBER OF CARDS IN THE DECK.

23 A GROUP OF PEOPLE MADE A HERO SANDWICH THAT MEASURED A WHOPPING 241 FEET (73 M).

24 THERE WAS A CHOCOLATE SUNDAE THAT COST $25,000.

25 A MAN DIDN'T SLEEP AS HE RODE A FERRIS WHEEL FOR MORE THAN 24 HOURS STRAIGHT.

26 THE HIGHEST WAVE EVER SURFED WAS OVER 100 FEET (30 M) TALL.

27 A RABBIT'S TEETH USUALLY GROW BETWEEN 3 AND 5 INCHES (7.6 TO 12.7 CM) EACH YEAR.

28 CHEFS AT A UNIVERSITY IN MASSACHUSETTS, U.S.A., MADE A STEW THAT WEIGHED 6,656 POUNDS (3,019 KG).

29 EACH YEAR, ABOUT 50 PEOPLE IN THE UNITED STATES ARE STRUCK BY LIGHTNING AND LIVE TO TELL ABOUT IT.

30 THE WORLD'S LARGEST SCHOOL HAS AN ENROLLMENT OF MORE THAN 44,000 STUDENTS.

CHECK YOUR ANSWERS ON PAGES 175–176.

Pick a Number ...

1 Which is the only number that is twice the sum of its digits?

a. 18
b. 27
c. 124
d. There is no such number.

2 Which of these metro areas is the most populated, with more than 8.9 million people?

a. Paris, France
b. Los Angeles, California, U.S.A.
c. Tokyo, Japan
d. Mexico City, Mexico

3 Which number in China is considered unlucky because its name sounds like the word for "death" in Chinese?

a. 2
b. 4
c. 67.1825
d. a zom-billion

4 True or false? From 1 to 1,000, the only written numeral with an *a* in it is the word "thousand."

5 In the expression "I'll see you in a *jiffy*," how long is a jiffy?

a. 1/100th of a second
b. 1 minute
c. 9 minutes
d. 8 hours

6 True or false?
$12 + 3 - 4 + 5 + 67 + 8 + 9 = 98$

7 In which number are the letters of its written form in alphabetical order?

a. 40
b. 64
c 76
d. 99

8 Which number is also known as *naught*, *zilch*, and *zip*?

a. 0
b. 9
c. 100
d. There is no such number.

9 True or false? The opposite sides of a die always add up to 7.

10 How many hexagons are on an official soccer ball?

a. 5
b. 6
c. 20
d. none

11 Assuming one second per count, how long would it take you to count to one billion?

a. 3 hours
b. 3 days
c. 32 days
d. 32 years

THE AMAZING HUMAN MACHINE

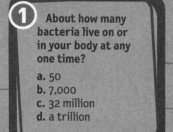

1 About how many bacteria live on or in your body at any one time?

a. 50
b. 7,000
c. 32 million
d. a trillion

2 About how many different species of organisms live in an adult's intestines at one time?

a. Zero. Everything gets digested.
b. 1
c. 500
d. 100,000

3 How many fingers do most cartoon characters have on one hand?

a. 3
b. 4
c. 5
d. 6

4 On average, how much taller are you in the morning than in the evening?

a. 0.4 inch (1 cm)
b. 1 inch (2.5 cm)
c. 3 inches (7.6 cm)
d. 12 inches (30.5 cm)

5 In your lifetime, how many spiders will you eat while sleeping?

a. Zero. Spiders typically don't let themselves get eaten.
b. 4 to 8
c. 10 to 15
d. a thousand

6 Sudden exposure to _____ causes between 10 and 35 percent of the population to sneeze.

a. bright light
b. coffee
c. tissues
d. chores

7 What is the largest number of children born to one woman in a lifetime?

a. 4
b. 18
c. 69
d. 101

8 How many times a day does the average person pass gas?

a. 1
b. 14
c. 134
d. No one knows because know no one will tell.

9 **True or false?** The only place where organisms cannot live on your body is in your eyelashes.

10 The human heart can create enough pressure to squirt blood this far.

a. 14 inches (36 cm)
b. 2 feet (61 cm)
c. 30 feet (9 m)
d. 1 mile (1.6 km)

11 How often do people shed their entire layer of outer skin cells?

a. every 2 to 4 weeks
b. every 6 months
c. once a year
d. every time they watch a scary movie

12 The average human body contains enough carbon to make how many pencils?

a. 1
b. 150
c. 900
d. 10,000

CHECK YOUR ANSWERS ON PAGES 175–176.

To Infinity...
and Beyond!

1 When daredevil Felix Baumgartner skydived from the edge of Earth's atmosphere and parachuted back to Earth, about how far did he travel?

a. 24 miles (39 km)
b. 432 miles (695 km)
c. 5,728 miles (9,218 km)
d. To infinity

2 How long would it take to get to Mars on a modern spacecraft?

a. 25 days, if the traffic's not bad
b. 150 to 300 days, depending on how close Earth is to Mars
c. a little over 10 years
d. 23 years, with the right kind of rocket

3 Which is the farthest distance any human has ever been from Earth?

a. 6.6 miles (11 km)
b. 23 miles (37 km)
c. 1,324 miles (2,131 km)
d. 248,655 miles (400,171 km)

4 How many Earths could fit inside Jupiter?

a. 2
b. 17
c. 200
d. more than 1,000

5 What travels 186,282 miles (299,792 km) per second?

a. a comet
b. a spacecraft
c. light
d. an asteroid

6 What is the record number of days spent in space by a human?

a. 2
b. 28
c. 438
d. 1,825

7 True or false? Up to 98 percent of astronauts' urine can get recycled back into drinking water on the International Space Station.

8 What is the longest amount of time spent by a human on the moon?

a. 34 minutes   b. 8 hours
c. about 75 hours   d. 5 days

9 How old was the oldest person to ever travel in space?

a. 24 years old   b. 53 years old
c. 77 years old   d. 101 years old

10 About how wide was the asteroid that may have led to the dinosaurs' extinction?

a. as wide as a soccer goal, about 24 feet
   (7.3 m)
b. as wide as five football fields, about
   500 yards (457 m)
c. as wide as 26 Great Pyramids of Egypt,
   about 6 miles (10 km)
d. as wide as Taiwan, about 106 to 186 miles
   (171 to 299 km)

11 How long did it take for Apollo 11—the first spacecraft to land on the moon—to reach the moon?

a. 3 days   b. 1 week
c. 1 month   d. 1 year

12 What is the record for the longest human space walk?

a. 32 minutes   b. 24 hours
c. 8 hours,   d. 72 hours,
   56 minutes   45 minutes

By the Numbers

1 If you attend school for 6 hours a day and 180 days a year, how many hours will you have been in school by the time you complete kindergarten to grade 12?

a. 84
b. 380
c. 14,040
d. Too many!

2 How many holes are there in a Wiffle ball?

a. 3: 2 for your fingers and 1 for your thumb
b. 8
c. 24
d. 120

3 In what year was Popeye the Sailor Man created?

a. 1899
b. 1929
c. 1945
d. 1990

POPEYE

4 How long is a bowling alley?

a. 3 feet (1 m)
b. 60 feet (18 m)
c. 200 feet (61 m)
d. 500 feet (152 m)

5 Which three numbers are used as the area code in telephone numbers in movies and television but not in real telephone numbers?

a. 222
b. 555
c. 845
d. 911

6 About how much does a million dollars weigh if it is all in one-dollar bills?

a. 1 pound (0.45 kg)
b. 500 pounds (228 kg)
c. 2,200 pounds (998 kg)
d. 1 million pounds (453,592 kg)

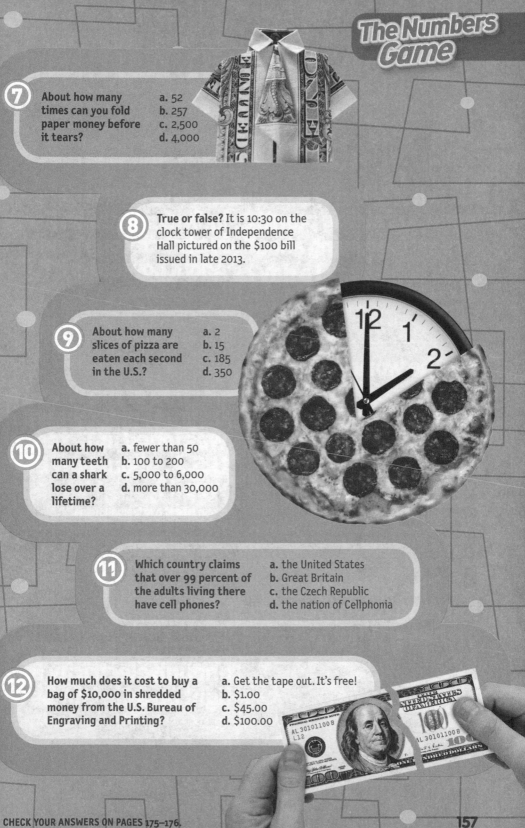

7 About how many times can you fold paper money before it tears?

a. 52
b. 257
c. 2,500
d. 4,000

8 **True or false?** It is 10:30 on the clock tower of Independence Hall pictured on the $100 bill issued in late 2013.

9 About how many slices of pizza are eaten each second in the U.S.?

a. 2
b. 15
c. 185
d. 350

10 About how many teeth can a shark lose over a lifetime?

a. fewer than 50
b. 100 to 200
c. 5,000 to 6,000
d. more than 30,000

11 Which country claims that over 99 percent of the adults living there have cell phones?

a. the United States
b. Great Britain
c. the Czech Republic
d. the nation of Cellphonia

12 How much does it cost to buy a bag of $10,000 in shredded money from the U.S. Bureau of Engraving and Printing?

a. Get the tape out. It's free!
b. $1.00
c. $45.00
d. $100.00

CHECK YOUR ANSWERS ON PAGES 175–176.

Wonders of NATURE

1 What is the fastest-growing plant on Earth, growing about 35 inches (91 cm) a day?

a. kudzu vine
b. bamboo
c. spider plant
d. dandelion

2 The oldest individual tree on Earth is a bristlecone pine. About how old is it?

a. 100 years old
b. 586 years old
c. 5,062 years old
d. 1.5 million years old

3 The world's largest beaver dam is so big, it can be located using Google Earth. How big is it?

a. two times the length of Hoover Dam
b. three times the length of a tennis court
c. five times the size of a bathtub
d. the same size as Yankee Stadium in New York

4 One of the world's largest spiderwebs was found in Texas, U.S.A. About how big was it?

a. the size of two football fields
b. the size of two extra-large pizzas with mosquito toppings
c. the size of Loch Ness
d. the size of the Great Wall of China

5 The convergent ladybug can have 13 of these. What are they?

a. pairs of legs
b. eyes
c. layers of wings
d. spots

6 True or false? Electric eels generate enough electricity to light up a Christmas tre

The Numbers Game

7 **What is Earth's loudest animal?**

a. the screech owl
b. the elephant
c. the blue whale
d. the laughing hyena

8 **True or false? Some species of seals can hold their breath underwater for an hour.**

9 **About how many glasses of milk can the average cow produce in its lifetime?**

a. 240
b. 720
c. 700,000
d. 200,000

10 **How big was the world's largest jack-o'-lantern?**

a. 24 pounds (11 kg)
b. 200 pounds (91 kg)
c. 1,811 pounds (821 kg)
d. 2,345 pounds (1,064 kg)

12 **About how many quills does a porcupine have?**

a. 700
c. 10,000
b. 1,400
d. 30,000

11 **How fast can a woodpecker peck?**

a. 20 times a second
b. 150 times a second
c. 300 times a second
d. 850 times a second

That's Entertainment!

1 In what year did Mickey Mouse appear in his first movie?
a. 1982
b. 1947
c. 1928
d. 1896

2 About how many hours a week does the average teenager spend playing video games?
a. 9
b. 12
c. 20
d. 50

3 How much did a rare 1914 Babe Ruth baseball card recently sell for?
a. $24
b. $300
c. $8,900
d. $450,000

4 With more than $760,000,000 in box-office sales, what is the top-selling movie of all time?
a. *Finding Nemo*
b. *Avatar*
c. *Harry Potter and the Half-Blood Prince*
d. *The Twilight Saga: New Moon*

5 More than 51 million Americans enjoy this hobby in their leisure time.
a. duck calling
b. doing the chicken dance
c. bird-watching
d. painting birds

MAKO SHARK

6 In bowling, what does a Golden Turkey refer to?
a. a full game of gutter balls
b. nine strikes in a row
c. the guy in the next lane who cheats
d. a strike

7 **True or false?** Some people once spent 384 hours playing Monopoly in a moving elevator.

MONOPOLY

8 What U.S. sport offered fans tickets to its championship game for $2,600 each?
a. football
b. baseball
c. hockey
d. thumb wrestling

9 Americans spend about $22 billion a year on these.
a. toys
b. books
c. parades
d. bicycles

10 A fisherman reeled in a mako shark weighing 1,323.5 pounds (600 kg). How long did it take to reel in this monster of a fish?
a. 23 minutes
b. 1 hour 5 minutes
c. 2 hours 30 minutes
d. He's still trying to reel him in!

11 What U.S. national monument gets almost 6 million visitors each year?
a. the Lincoln Memorial in Washington, D.C.
b. the Statue of Liberty in New York
c. the Liberty Bell in Pennsylvania
d. Mount Rushmore in South Dakota

GAME SHOW

ULTIMATE NUMBERS CHALLENGE

1 How many miles of bookshelves line the U.S. Library of Congress, one of the world's largest libraries?
- **a.** 5 miles (8 km)
- **b.** 84 miles (135 km)
- **c.** 200 miles (322 km)
- **d.** 838 miles (1,349 km)

2 TRUE OR FALSE?
The average person speaks 600 words per day.

3 TRUE OR FALSE?
When Apollo 11 landed on the moon, it had only about 30 seconds of fuel left.

4 On average, how many hours does a sloth sleep each day?
- **a.** 2 to 4 hours
- **b.** 6 to 8 hours
- **c.** 15 to 20 hours
- **d.** 22 to 24 hours

5 Being on "cloud nine" means you are _____.
- **a.** really happy
- **b.** very rich
- **c.** dressed in your best
- **d.** flying at an altitude of 9,000 feet (2,743.2 m)

6 How wide is the world's biggest flower, the giant Rafflesia—also called the stinking corpse lily?
- **a.** 5 inches (12.7 cm)
- **b.** 12 inches (30.48 cm)
- **c.** 39 inches (99.06 cm)
- **d.** 50 feet (15.24 m)

7 With five million square feet (464,515,200 m²) of shopping area and room for 2,350 stores, what is the world's biggest mall?
- **a.** Mall of America, U.S.A.
- **b.** South China Mall, China
- **c.** Dubai Mall, United Arab Emirates
- **d.** Istanbul Cevahir, Turkey

8 About how many Earths would fit inside the sun?
a. 10
b. 500
c. 1 million
d. 6,000

9 **TRUE OR FALSE?**
When scientists tested 60 people's belly buttons, they found 2,368 different species of bacteria.

10 How many calories can a 150-pound (68-kg) person burn by salsa dancing for an hour?
a. None   b. 396
c. 1,500   d. 2,400

11 What is the speed of the fastest pitch ever recorded in baseball?
a. 22.8 miles an hour (36.7 km/h)
b. 54 miles an hour (87 km/h)
c. 105.1 miles an hour (169.1 km/h)
d. 300 miles an hour (483 km/h)

12 What does the Roman numeral MMDCXLVII mean?
a. 213
b. 1,028
c. 2,647
d. It's time for the Olympics again.

13 About how many people could fit inside a blue whale's mouth?
a. 1
b. 5
c. 100
d. 250

14 Iceland is one of the countries with the largest Internet use. Which percent of the population surfs the Net?
a. 25 percent
b. 50 percent
c. 90 percent
d. 100 percent

15 **ULTIMATE BRAIN BUSTER**
CAN YOU NAME THIS GAME, WHICH EARNS AROUND $300 MILLION EACH YEAR DESPITE BEING FREE TO PLAY?

CHECK YOUR ANSWERS ON PAGES 175–176.

ANSWERS

Pet Pals

You've Gotta Be Kitten Me!
pages 10–11

1. c
2. **True.** A cat can sleep 12.5 hours a day or more.
3. d
4. b
5. c
6. a
7. b
8. d
9. a
10. c
11. d
12. b

Doggone Fun!
pages 12–13

1. b
2. **False.** Dalmatian puppies are born with no spots at all.
3. **True.** From tiny teacup poodles to huge Great Danes, most adult dogs have about 320 bones and 42 teeth.
4. a
5. c
6. c
7. d
8. c
9. c
10. b
11. d
12. c

White House Pets,
pages 14–15

1. b
2. d
3. a
4. c
5. a
6. c
7. d
8. a
9. b
10. **True.** U.S. President George H. W. Bush's pet was Millie, who had puppies while at the White House, and Bush's son, President George W. Bush, kept one of Millie's puppies, Spotty.
11. **False.** Benjamin Harrison kept an opossum as a pet.
12. b

Pocket Pets,
pages 16–17

1. b
2. d
3. **True.** The biggest this species from northern Africa gets is 3 inches (8 cm) long.
4. a
5. c
6. **True.** These fuzzy pets can jump over 6 feet (1.8 m), and some pet chinchillas have jumped on top of their owners' refrigerators!
7. c
8. d. Humans domesticated the guinea pig about 3,000 years ago.
9. d
10. d
11. b
12. **True.** There are African, Asian, and Indian varieties, all living in arid habitats.

The X Factor:
Pet Edition,
pages 18–19

1. **True.** Twiggy the squirrel appeared on *America's Got Talent*, Season 7, as a water-skiing squirrel.
2. **True.** Metro, a retired racehorse, paints by having a paintbrush placed in his mouth as he bobs his head up and down.
3. **False.** Kame-chan is known for singing the theme song of the video game *The Legend of Zelda*.
4. **True.** Domingo Pianezzi trained his alpaca, Pisco, to surf with him.
5. **True.** The parrot, named Yosuke, passed the time waiting for its owner by singing.
6. **False.** Tillman's claim to fame is skateboarding and surfing.
7. **False.** Amadeus knows how to play pool.
8. **True.** Comet the goldfish appeared on *Good Morning America* and showed the world what a goldfish can do.
9. **True.** Mudslinger and Digger are also known as the Top Hogs.
10. **True.** Oolong had an unusually flat head, so balancing things was easy.
11. **True.** It can take many years to train a bear to look mean.
12. **True.** Chandi swept to fame by dancing ballet.
13. **True.** Miniature horses can be trained to be excellent guides for blind people.
14. **True.** The cat, named Kuzma, even wears a bow tie to work.
15. **True.** Einstein was born only 14 inches (35.6 cm) tall—too small to be safe around the bigger horses.
16. **False.** They hold the record for number of dogs jumping rope at one time.
17. **True.** There is a YouTube video of her making sounds that sound like "hello" and "I love you."
18. **True.** Goldfish, bettas, and oscars are popular fish to train to do tricks.
19. **True.** Mutley has his own scuba suit and also scubas with his companion cat.
20. **False.** Nora loves playing the piano.
21. **False.** Nugget can solve simple math problems, such as 6 + 6 and 4–3.
22. **True.** Ratatouille takes to the slopes in his hand-knit sweater and, of course, with his lift ticket.
23. **True.** He can also put dishes in the dishwasher and turn out the lights.
24. **True.** With a bit of training, bunnies can learn where to go.
25. **False.** Einstein was named because she is no birdbrain. She mimics on cue and makes more than 200 sounds, including words.
26. **False.** Sweet Pea is a talented dog.
27. **True.** Anastasia can even pop balloons in the air by biting them.
28. **True.** Pet Rocks were sold in the 1970s and even came with a training manual.
29. **False.** He had a flea circus in New York.
30. **True.** Champis herds sheep in a small village in Sweden.

Aquarium Antics,
pages 20–21

1. a
2. d
3. c
4. **True.** Angelfish can become quite aggressive and have been known to eat such aquarium mates as neon tetra fish.
5. c
6. b
7. c
8. **True.** The tank measures 26 feet (8 m) long and is about 100 times bigger than an average 10-gallon (38-L) tank.
9. a
10. a
11. b
12. a

Celebrity Pets,
pages 22–23

1. d
2. b
3. b
4. b
5. **False.** Only males have ever portrayed Lassie.
6. c
7. a
8. a
9. c
10. a
11. d

PHOTO CREDITS KEY: SS=Shutterstock, iS=iStockphoto, GI=Getty Images
Cover: (tl) Edith Layland/Dreamstime; (tr) Bob Elsdale/Kimball Stock; (cr) Chip Clark/NMNH/Smithsonian Institution; (bl) REX USA/Crollalanza; (br) Zigiz/Dreamstime; Background, cammep/SS; **Back Cover:** (tl) Anton Balazh/SS; (cr) Lightzoom/Dreamstime; Background, cammep/SS; **Spine:** Le-thuy Do/Dreamstime; **Front Matter:** 1 (tcr) Petrenko Andriy/SS; 1 (bc) ssuaphotos/SS; 1 (bcl) picturin/SS; 4, (tcr) Jaguar PS/SS; 4, (bcr) Robyn Butler/SS; 4, (cl) SergeyDV/SS; 4, (tl) Eduard Kyslynskyy/SS; 5, (bcl) Dan Breckwoldt/SS; 5, (tcr) Darla Hallmark/SS; 5, (tcl) homydesign/SS; 5, (bcr) Nomad_Soul/SS; 6, (cl) bluehand/SS; 7, (br) dutourdumonde/SS; **Pet Pals [8-25]:** 8-9, (main) Eduard Kyslynsky/SS; 10-11, (main) DenisNata/SS; 12, (bl) Yuri Kravchenko/SS; 12, (tr) kyokoliberty/SS; 13, (tr)

Game Show: Ultimate Pet Challenge, pages 24–25

1. a
2. **True.** However, it wasn't the cats themselves but the fleas in their coats that spread the plague.
3. c
4. c
5. b
6. a
7. b
8. **True.** It made its way across forests, hills, and rivers to find its family.
9. a
10. d
11. c
12. b
13. **True.** Lulu went back and forth between her owner and the street until she got help.
14. b
15. Scooby-Doo is a Great Dane.

SCORING

0–39

BARELY BARKING

Animals might not be your thing, but that's okay. Not everyone wants to be the next Jane Goodall, so there's nothing to howl about. You don't need to know all the facts about fur, fins, and feathers. Just be kind and considerate to the creatures we share the world with.

40–78

MIDDLE OF THE PACK

You're not the alpha dog, but you're no mutt, either. You definitely know quite a few tricks. You might not be ready to host your own animal show just yet, but you're on your way. And with a little more learning and practice, you'll soon be the top dog.

79–116

BEST IN SHOW

You are the king of the jungle, a real hot dog, and the cat's meow. From alligators to zebras—if it bellows or brays, you speak the language. Keep up the good work to stay ahead of the pack.

Big Ideas

Water Wonders, pages 28–29

1. **False.** Scientists have not made false teeth for sharks, but they have created prosthetic tails to help injured dolphins swim again.
2. b
3. c
4. d
5. a
6. **False.** Opportunity discovered evidence that there had once been water on Mars long ago.
7. b
8. a
9. c
10. d
11. a

Out of This World, pages 30–31

1. c
2. b
3. d
4. a
5. d
6. b
7. a
8. c
9. **False.** A water bag inside the space suit has a tube that goes inside the helmet so the astronaut can drink water.
10. **True.** A space walk usually lasts more than six hours, so the astronauts need this protection.
11. d

Gizmos, Gadgets, and Gear, pages 32–33

1. **False.** The 1960 election was the first time the candidates were on television. The television appearances helped Kennedy.
2. **False.** They lasted for 13.5 hours.
3. **True.** It was introduced in 2002. It can go around objects on the floor.
4. **True.** British inventor Arthur Paul Pedrick invented a number of useless inventions like this one.
5. **True.** Fakhri Raihaan of Indonesia set this record in 2013.
6. **True.** It got its name because it was waterproof, like a duck's feathers.
7. **False.** In 1902, the first lunchbox made for kids had a picture of children playing.
8. **True.** The staples were made of gold and had jewels on them.
9. **True.** A translation app on a smartphone can translate multiple languages.
10. **True.** The cord was attached to one end, and the designer thought it looked like a mouse's tail.
11. **True.** Soap was added around 1824 but was taken out around the 1940s.
12. **False.** It was made for the Swiss Army. Each new soldier got one.
13. **True.** Almost 75% of the people in the world have one or have access to one.
14. **False.** The watch was introduced in 1933, five years after Mickey's first movie.
15. **True.** The name is still used as a slang term today.

Taylor Hill/GI Entertainment/GI; 13, (bl) WOLF AVNI/SS; 14-15, (main) DanielW/SS; 16, (tr) Lepas/SS; 16, (br) Eric Isselee/SS; 16, (cl) margouillat photo/SS; 17, (tl) vovan/SS; 17, (br) Eric Isselee/SS; 20, (tl) Michaelboyer91/SS; 20 (bl) Photobank gallery/SS; 20, (tr) Copyright: Mariusz Niedzwiedzki; 20, (cr) serg_dibrova/SS; 21, (bl) bluehand/SS; 21, (cr) bluehand/SS; 22-23, (main) Ron Haviv/VII/ Corbis; 24, (br) WilleeCole/SS; 24, (tr) Eftyhia Mavri/SS; 24, (cl) Isselee/Dreamstime; 25, (br) Joe Seer/SS; 25, (bl-c) lalito/SS; 25, (bl-b) Axel Bueckert/SS; 25, (bl-a) bluehand/SS; 25, (tr) Eric Isselee/SS; 25, (bl-d) Andrey_Kuzmin/SS; 25, (tl) Steshkin Yevgeniy/SS; **Big Ideas [26-43]:** 26-27, (main) Capture Light/SS; 26-27, (main) HomeStudio/SS; 28, (c-c) Fedor Selivanov/SS; 28, (bl) SergeyDV/SS; 28, (c-d) Paul D Smith/SS; 28, (c-b) holbox/SS; 28, (c-a) Tupungato/SS; 28, (tr) Torsak Thammachote/SS; 29, (tl) AF archive/Alamy; 29, (br)

16. **True.** Dogs could hear the ultrasound waves, and the waves hurt their ears.
17. **False.** NASA engineer Lonnie Johnson invented the Super Soaker in 1989.
18. **True.** You can practice for the real spelling bee!
19. **False.** They were first sold in Atlantic City, New Jersey, U.S.A., in 1929.
20. **False.** It was invented in Toronto, Canada, in 2007, and played between the Windbreakers and the Fallen Leafs.
21. **True.** The modern version was put on rubber boots called galoshes in the 1920s but was invented in the 1890s.
22. **False.** The Kindle was not the first, but it was able to download content faster than other e-readers when it came out.
23. **False.** The light on the first flashlight flashed instead of staying on all the time.
24. **True.** It was added to the Oxford English Dictionary in 1986.
25. **False.** Spoons and forks were used in ancient times. The earliest record of a spork was from the late 1800s.
26. **False.** It was made for an airplane pilot so the pilot could operate the plane's controls and see a watch.
27. **True.** Scientist Nikola Tesla made the prediction in 1909. The Blackberry was used to send the first text messages in 1992.
28. **True.** The British government bought them for the Royal Air Force.
29. **True.** The name comes from the line "Open the pod bay doors, Hal."
30. **False.** Over 150 million systems have been sold.

On the Move, pages 34–35

1. b
2. **True.** Only 46 of the luxury cars were made.
3. d
4. c
5. a

6. b
7. b
8. **True.** The track coach who made these waffle soles founded Nike a few years later.
9. b
10. **True.** Utah State University developed the Personal Vacuum Assisted Climber. The motor is worn like a backpack. Two suction pads let the wearer climb any surface. The device is being used by the military.
11. d

Ideas for Tomorrow, pages 36–37

1. c
2. a
3. b
4. c
5. a
6. d
7. a
8. a
9. **False.** Scientists can use virtual reality to beam an avatar, but they can't beam real people and things yet.
10. b
11. c
12. **False.** Even if the jet pack is successful, it won't be legal in crowded areas such as cities.

Smart Animals, pages 38–39

1. d
2. **True.** A crow puts a nut on the road. After a car has broken the shell, the crow waits for traffic to stop to pick up its food.
3. b
4. a
5. **True.** This may be the first time an animal has used a tool to communicate.
6. a
7. **False.** They use stones to seal the entrance of their nests to protect their eggs.

8. d
9. b
10. d
11. c

Map Mania! You Saw It Here First, pages 40–41

1. Kites: China
2. Returning boomerangs: Australia
3. Electric guitars: United States
4. Breath Mints: Egypt
5. Pizza: Italy
6. Flushing toilets: United Kingdom
7. Velcro: Switzerland
8. Yo-yos: Greece
9. Hot-air balloons: France
10. Space satellites: Russia/U.S.S.R.
11. Chess: India

Game Show: Ultimate Big Ideas Challenge, pages 42–43

1. c
2. d
3. a
4. b
5. a
6. **False.** Two men, Brian Jones and Bertrand Piccard, went around the world in a balloon in 1999.
7. **True.** The inventors hope that people will use the fork to learn to eat more slowly.
8. a
9. c
10. a
11. **True.** Scientists have seen adult females, but not males, teaching the young.
12. d
13. b
14. a
15. d

SCORING

0–37

NO BIG DEAL

You may not have thought much about the wacky, wonderful, and oh-so-useful things that are all around you. So take off your scratch-resistant sunglasses and turn off your iPod! You might want to do some reading to find out more about all the inventive minds out there.

38–75

THE WHEELS ARE SPINNING

You know quite a few things about inventions, inventors, and gadgets. You like to find out how things work. Keep filling your mind with awesome ideas and one day you might be on the front page of the best gadget blogs and magazines.

76–112

EUREKA!

Your brain is a-stormin'! You're techno-savvy and know about the greatest gadgets now and for the future. In fact, a number of those inventions of tomorrow just might turn out to be yours. Keep the lights burning and the wheels turning!

Borisoff/SS; 30-31, (main) NASA/Science Faction/GI; 34, (bl) Vacclav/SS; 34, (cl) SeanPavonePhoto/SS; 34, (tr) dutourdumonde/SS; 35, (cr) Otis Imboden/National Geographic/GI; 35, (bl) eli_asenova/iStock; 35, (tc) Randy Jolly/Aero Graphics, Inc./CORBIS; 36-37, (c) Robert Mandel/SS; 38, (cl) ericlefrancais/SS; 38, (br) AKauroraPhotos/iS; 38, (tl) Hill2k/SS; 38, (cr) fjdelvalle/iS; 39, (tr) Aneese/iS; 39, (br) aodaodaodaod/SS; 39, (tl) vblinov/SS; 40, (tc) Graeme Dawes/SS; 40, (cl) S_E/SS; 40, (cr) StudioSmart/SS; 40, (br) Katstudio/SS; 40, (bl) MartiniDry/SS; 41, (cr) joppo/SS; 41, (bl) Sumikophoto/SS; 41, (bc) EduardHarkonen/iS; 41, (tl) extradeda/SS; 41, (tr) KirVKV/SS; 41, (br) Sergey Peterman/SS; 42, (br) EddWestmacott/iS; 42, (cl) EpicStockMedia/SS; 43, (bc-b) Sergiy Kuzmin/SS; 43, (cl) ssuaphotos/SS; 43, (bc-a) Supertrooper/SS; 43, (bc-d) Matteo Gabrieli/SS; 43, (tl) Paul Orr/SS; 43, (bc-c) ventdusud/SS; **Pop Culture [44-59]:** 44-45, (main)

Pop Culture

Toy Stories,
pages 46–47

1. c
2. **True.** HexBugs react to sounds, light, and pressure.
3. c
4. d
5. c
6. d
7. b
8. d
9. c
10. **True.** Astronauts on the Apollo 8 mission used Silly Putty to hold down floating tools.
11. **False.** They were called Matchbox cars because they fit inside a matchbox.
12. b

Music to Your Ears,
pages 48–49

1. b
2. d
3. c
4. **True.** Before moving to Hollywood to become pop stars, the boys were lacing up their skates in Minnesota.
5. b
6. c
7. d
8. **False.** Adam Levine is the lead singer of Maroon 5.
9. b
10. d
11. a
12. a

The Book Club,
pages 50–51

1. c
2. d
3. b
4. c
5. **False.** *The Hunger Games* takes place in a nation known as Panem.
6. a
7. a
8. **False.** Lemony Snicket is the narrator of the stories.
9. b
10. **True.** Apophis is a giant serpent who is into destruction.
11. a
12. a

Tons of Toons,
pages 52–53

1. **True.** The cat-and-mouse duo won 7 Oscars.
2. **False.** The book is titled *Da Rules*.
3. **False.** Plankton is named Sheldon.
4. **True.** Ocho is a nice 8-bit spider, unless he is angered.
5. **False.** Frosty is brought to life by a magic top hat.
6. **True.** O.W.C.A is the best they could come up with.
7. **False.** King Julien is a bossy lemur.
8. **False.** *Toy Story* was the first feature-length movie created with computers.
9. **False.** The main characters are two brothers, Edward and Alphonse, who are not twins.
10. **False.** Ethan and Peaches are not related.
11. **False.** Mordecai and Rigby work as groundskeepers at a park.
12. **True.** The head honcho at the AVL is Silas Ramsbottom.
13. **True.** Bugs's Brooklyn accent identifies him as a true New Yorker.
14. **False.** Fred is nicknamed Twinkletoes because of his bowling style.
15. **False.** The Jetsons' pet is a futuristic *dog* named Astro.
16. **False.** Scooby's nephew is named Scrappy-Doo.
17. **True.** Garfield has been hooked on lasagna since he was born.
18. **False.** Russell is a member of the Wilderness Explorers.
19. **False.** Dexter's mom has no idea her son has a secret laboratory in the house.
20. **False.** Sally is Charlie Brown's sister.
21. **True.** Buzz and Delete help Hacker in his quest to overthrow Motherboard.
22. **False.** Popeye is the cartoon character who often uses this statement.
23. **False.** Luigi's favorite kind of car is the Ferrari.
24. **False.** Comedian Steve Carell voices Gru, the villain turned hero in *Despicable Me*.
25. **False.** Aang is the name of the last airbender.
26. **True.** Bullwinkle plays quarterback for the Wossamotta U. football team.
27. **False.** A *meteor* hit Ginormica, making her grow 49 feet tall.
28. **True.** Before turning into the Ice King, he was a normal, glasses-wearing man.
29. **False.** Porky Pig, not Daffy Duck, often uses this famous sign-off.
30. **True.** Wile E. Coyote uses many Acme products, including a giant rubber band and jet-powered tennis shoes.

Famous Pairs,
pages 54–55

1. c
2. c
3. d
4. b
5. **True.** Pinky and the Brain are laboratory mice who live in Acme Labs.
6. c
7. d
8. **False.** Mario and Luigi are brothers who work as plumbers.
9. a
10. c
11. a
12. a

Heroes and Heroines,
pages 56–57

1. **True.** The movie starred Adam West as the caped wonder.
2. **False.** Shaggy and Scooby-Doo's favorite treat is Scooby snacks.
3. **False.** The power ring is fueled by willpower.
4. **True.** Storm even led the X-Men for a while in the comic books.
5. **True.** Merida uses her archery skills and bravery to undo an evil curse.
6. **False.** The correct name for Aragorn's sword is Andúril.
7. **True.** Han pilots the ship with his Wookiee friend, Chewbacca.
8. **True.** Superman got Krypto when he was Superboy in 1955.
9. **False.** This quote is from the book *How to Train Your Dragon* by Cressida Cowell.
10. **True.** Each character in the series has a unique Patronus.
11. **False.** Indy despises snakes.
12. **True.** Matt Murdock, aka Daredevil, was blinded in an accident as a child.
13. **True.** Jodie Jenkins is the main character of the book and is super-strong.
14. **False.** He is a clown fish.
15. **True.** The Flash is called the Fastest Man Alive for good reason.
16. **False.** Flint's pet monkey's name is Steve.
17. **True.** The evil alien costume even tries to control Spider-Man's body.
18. **False.** Optimus Prime leads the Autobots against the Decepticons.
19. **True.** Hermione actually said, "Books! And cleverness! There are more important things—friendship and bravery."
20. **True.** The Omnitrix allows Ben to turn into alien creatures to save the day.
21. **False.** Casey Jones is a hero for giving up his life to save others during a train accident in 1900.
22. **True.** Green Arrow uses his wealth and marksmanship to protect Star City.
23. **True.** The dog was an Alaskan malamute.
24. **True.** In the books, Leia becomes a powerful Jedi.
25. **True.** Wolverine was born in or before 1897, but his mutant power slows his aging.
26. **False.** Tonto is the Comanche man who accompanies the Lone Ranger.
27. **False.** The ring that Bilbo finds allows him to become invisible.
28. **True.** After she was injured, Barbara became "Oracle," and she helped Batman with her computing skills.
29. **True.** Finn is a boy who wants to be a hero, and Jake is his dog.
30. **False.** She-Hulk is the cousin of the Incredible Hulk.

Archives du 7e Art/20th Century Fox/Photos 12/Alamy; 46, (tr) David Brabiner/Alamy; 46, (tl) skodonnell/iS; 46, (cr) Lightzoom/Dreamstime; 46, (bl) Catherine Lane/iS; 47, (cr) Franck Fotos/Alamy; 47, (bc) martin lauricella/Alamy; 48-49, (main) XiXinXing/SS; 50, (tr) Scott O'Dell/Houghton Mifflin Harcourt; 50, (cl) WARNER BROS/Ronald/AgeFotostock; 50, (br) Jasper Fforde/Houghton Mifflin Harcourt; 51, (bl) Amy Sussman/Stringer/GI; 51, (tr) AF archive/Alamy; 54, (bl) ABC Photo Archives/Disney ABC Television Group/GI; 54, (tr) AF archive/Alamy; 54, (cr) AF archive/Alamy; 55, (tr) Cindy Ord/GI Entertainment/GI; 55, (bl) Moviestore Collection/Moviestore collection Ltd/Alamy; 58, (br) Debby Wong/SS; 58, (cl) s_bukley/SS; 58, (tr) skodonnell/iS; 59, (bcr) JLC/ZOJ WENN Photos/Newscom; 59, (cl) Richard Harbaugh/Disney ABC Television Group/GI; 59, (bl) RJAce1014/SS; 59, (tr-d) BrendanHunter/iS; 59, (tr-b) Jason Kempin/

1. c
2. a
3. a

4. d
5. b
6. **False.** *The Lost Hero* is the first book in this series. *The Lightning Thief* is the first book in the Percy Jackson and the Olympians series.
7. c
8. d
9. c

10. **False.** A RipStik is a type of skateboard.
11. d
12. b
13. a
14. b
15. c

SCORING

0–40

TUNED OUT

Pop culture doesn't get you moving? No worries. Besides, you're too busy investigating the world in other ways. Explore and enjoy the interests that get *your* blood pumping. Dancing to the beat of your own drummer makes you special.

41–81

TUNING UP

You are moving up the charts! You know what's in and what's out. But keep your eyes and ears open. The world of entertainment moves pretty fast. You never know who or what will become the newest sensation!

82–123

TUNED IN

You know what's going on! You've got the info on the hit makers, toy makers, top toons, and everything else. Remember that today's trends are often tomorrow's classics. Keep on keeping up!

Wild WORLD

Untamed!
pages 62–63

1. b
2. **True.** Special bones allow the tarsier to perform this freaky feat.
3. c
4. **False.** A male mosquito has a modified mouth allowing it to feed only on plant juices. Only female mosquitoes bite humans.
5. a
6. b
7. **True.** Both humans and giraffes, as well as most mammals, have seven vertebrae in their neck.
8. a

9. c
10. b
11. d

Plant Party,
pages 64–65

1. c
2. **True.** In Zimbabwe, an ancient baobab tree is large enough to contain 40 people inside its hollow trunk!
3. b
4. a
5. c
6. b
7. b
8. **True.** The mushroom known as the truffle can cost between $800 and $1,500 per pound!
9. c
10. **False.** Unripe green tomatoes are eaten by lots of people.
11. d

Off the Deep End,
pages 66–67

1. c
2. **True.** It won the unfortunate award in 2013.
3. a
4. d
5. b
6. **True.** The weird phenomenon is called a "brinicle," a combination of "brine" and "icicle."
7. c
8. a
9. b
10. c
11. b

City Critters,
pages 68–69

1. a
2. c

GI Entertainment/GI; 59, (tr-c) Jaguar PS/SS; 59, (tr-a) Catherine Lane/iS; **Wild World [60-83]:** 60-61, (main) Gleb Tarro/SS; 62, (cr) Natursports/SS; 62, (bl) Sergey Uryadnikov/SS; 62, (tl) haveseen/SS; 63, (bcl) Maxim Petrichuk/SS; 63, (br) Robyn Butler/SS; 63, (tr) E. O./SS; 63, (cl) Eric Isselee/SS; 64-65, (main) Cathy Keifer/SS; 66 (tl) Kerryn Parkinson/NORFANZ Founding Parties; 66, (br) Imeh Akpanudosen/GI Entertainment/GI; 67, (br) bluehand/SS; 67, (tr) Wong Hock weng/SS; 68-69, (main) anatolypareev/SS; 70-71, (main) Anton_Ivanov/SS; 72-73, (main) Maria Skaldina/SS; 74, (c) JFunk/SS; 74, (bl) jeeaa.CHC/SS; 74, (tc) PdaMai/SS; 74, (br) Carsten Peter/Speleoresearch & Films/National Geographic/GI; 75, (tc) Reinhard Dirscherl/Visuals Unlimited/Corbis; 75, (bc) Inc/SS; 75, (cr) Steven Gill/SS; 78, (cr) NASA and The Hubble Heritage Team/NASA; 78, (tl) Sailorr/SS; 78, (bl) Igor Zh./SS; 78, (cl) Jan Kaliciak/SS; 79, (tl)

3. **True.** Rats harbor or transmit more than 40 diseases, including rabies, typhus, and the deadly plague of the 14th century, also known as the Black Death.
4. **a**
5. **c**
6. **d**
7. **False.** Contrary to popular belief, raccoons sometimes put their food in water because they use food as bait in foraging for aquatic animals.
8. **b**
9. **a**
10. **b**
11. **b**

Antarctic Chill!
pages 70–71

1. **b**
2. **d**
3. **c**
4. **a**
5. **False.** Antarctica is very windy, with some winds reaching more than 150 miles an hour (241 km/h).
6. **c**
7. **c**
8. **b**
9. **True.** Scientists believe that the Antarctic was once joined with South America, Africa, India, and Australia in one large continent.
10. **c**
11. **a**

Equator Navigator,
pages 72–73

1. **d**
2. **False.** Equatorial locations actually experience the fastest sunrises and sunsets, each taking only minutes.
3. **c**
4. **b**
5. **True.** If you are at the Equator, you are moving at nearly 1,000 miles an hour (1,600 km/h). Your speed decreases as you move toward the North or South Pole.
6. **d**
7. **b**
8. **c**
9. **b**
10. **False.** Many, but not all, places at the Equator are hot and humid. The elevation of Mount Kilimanjaro creates a climate with cool, dry weather.
11. **b**
12. **b**

Map Mania!
Nature Makes Its Mark!
pages 74–75

1. **a**
2. **c**
3. **False.** While it is true that Old Faithful's eruptions are predictable, they actually occur within a range of about 60 to 110 minutes.

4. **b**
5. **a**
6. **d**
7. **c**
8. Arches National Park, **G—Utah, U.S.A.**
9. Queen's Head, **B—Taiwan**
10. Old Faithful, **A—Wyoming, U.S.A.**
11. Cave of Crystals, **E—Chihuahuan Desert, Mexico**
12. Quintana Roo, **C—Yucatán Peninsula**
13. Iguazu Falls, **D—border of Brazil and Argentina**
14. Shark Bay, **F—western coast of Australia**

Destination: Wild Side!
pages 76–77

1. **False.** Mount Erebus in Antarctica is the southernmost active volcano on Earth.
2. **True.** One explorer described descending into the cave as "like climbing an inverted Mount Everest."
3. **True.** Though much more frequently 50 years ago than today, polar bears still occasionally visit Iceland.
4. **False.** Stretching over 1,600 miles (2,600 km), this reef system is off the coast of Queensland, Australia.
5. **False.** The largest bamboo plant in the world is in China.
6. **False.** The Dead Sea is too salty to drink, with a salt content six times higher than the ocean's.
7. **True.** The duck-billed platypus and the echidna, the only mammals to lay eggs, are found in Australia.
8. **False.** Chile is hilly, with mountains covering almost 80% of its surface.
9. **False.** Measuring about 2,180 miles (3,508 km) in length, the Appalachian Trail is located in the eastern part of U.S.A.
10. **True.** Both big cats are endangered and are protected in India's wilderness areas.
11. **True.** The Vasyugan Swamp in Russia is almost 20% wider than Switzerland.
12. **False.** Indonesia, located north of Australia, has more volcanoes than any other country.
13. **True.** The elevation of Death Valley is at 282 feet (86 m) below sea level.
14. **True.** Peru wants to protect these plants and has set up special areas for them called reserves.
15. **True.** At night, visitors also look for nocturnal creatures, such as the aardvark and the bush baby.
16. **True.** The point lies near the town of Kyle, North Dakota, U.S.A., and is roughly 1,000 miles (1,600 km) from the nearest coast.
17. **True.** This temperate rain forest is located on the coast of Canada's British Columbia.
18. **False.** Death Valley, in California, U.S.A., had the hottest day ever with temperatures at 134°F (56.7°C).
19. **False.** The branches are the Blue Nile and the White Nile.
20. **False.** The Galápagos Islands are home to the largest turtle species. The smallest is found in South Africa.
21. **True.** Sweden has some of the most forested land of all European countries.
22. **True.** The Uvs Lake Basin in

northwestern Mongolia has recorded temperatures as low as –72°F (–58°C).
23. **True.** Located in southern Africa, Botswana is an area of spectacular natural beauty and rich animal life.
24. **False.** The water in the Don Juan Pond in Antarctica is the saltiest.
25. **False.** Mount Olympus, a real mountain in Greece, is famous because it's the legendary home of the Greek gods.
26. **True.** The massive glacier is called Lambert Glacier and is located in Antarctica.
27. **False.** Easter Island is a Polynesian island located in the Pacific Ocean and is a special territory of Chile.
28. **True.** This impressive waterfall plunges to a maximum drop of about 355 feet (108 m).
29. **True.** Due to two different climates, the Andes between Argentina and Chile are divided into the Dry Andes and the Wet Andes.
30. **True.** During periods of high migration, gazelles, zebras, and other grazing animals blanket the Tanzanian landscape as far as the eye can see.

Out of This World!
pages 78–79

1. **c**
2. **c**
3. **a.** The canyon is called Mariner Valley.
4. **a**
5. **False.** Because it appeared to move swiftly, it was named after a Roman god, Mercury, who was known for his quickness.
6. **c**
7. **True.** But don't worry, Earth doesn't wobble so much that we would ever notice it.
8. **d**
9. **a**
10. **a**
11. **d**

Windy Weather,
pages 80–81

1. **b**
2. **d**
3. **True.** Giant dust storms commonly sweep across the planet.
4. **b**
5. **b**
6. **c**
7. **a**
8. **True.** Winds reached a speed of 318 miles an hour (511 km/h).
9. **a**
10. **c**
11. **d**
12. **True.** These flame-throwing tornadoes, called fire whirls, can be 50 feet (15 m) wide and as tall as a 40-story building.

maogg/iS; 79 (cr) Ammit Jack/SS; 79, (bl) Anonymous/NASA/AP Worldwide; 80-81, (main) cholder/SS; 82, (br) Brennan Linsley/ Associated Press; 82, (bl) Dennis Donohue/SS; 82, (cl) AlessandroZocc/SS; 83, (bc-b) Sergey Krasnoshchokov/SS; 83, (cr) picturin/SS; 83, (br-d) Tony Campbell/SS; 83, (br-c) Hotshotsworldwide/Dreamstime; 83, (br-a) MicheleBoiero/SS; 83, (tl) Predrag Vuckovic; **Sports Challenge [84-105]:** 84-85, (main) Marko Rupena/SS; 86-87, (main) Sergei Bachlakov/Dreamstime; 90, (bl) tkachuk/SS; 90, (br) Ken Durden/SS; 90, (tc) Vladimir Zhuravlev/Dreamstime; 91, (tc) trentham/Dreamstime; 91, (bl) Laura Stone/Dreamstime; 91, (br) Dmitry Burlakov/SS; 91, (br) Kevin R. Morris/Corbis; 92, (bl) Featureflash/SS; 92, (tr) Jerry Coli/Dreamstime; 92, (cl) Celso Pupo rodrigues/ Dreamstime; 93, (br) Domenic Gareri/SS; 93, (tr) Ron Foster Sharif/SS; 93, (cl) Debby Wong/SS; 94-95, (main) Jianbinglee/Dreamstime;

6. b
7. **True.** Pictures from the town showed
   everything from cars to houses covered
   in spider silk.
8. b
9. a
10. b
11. **True.** The plant that the cow ate was
    called white snakeroot.
12. b
13. a

14. **False.** Deserts
    are found on
    every continent,
    including Asia.
15. c

SCORING

0–49

LOST IN THE WILDERNESS

You probably find all the
adventure you need on television,
on the Internet, or in books. But
you should get outside and feed
your wild side, too!

50–99

FINDING YOUR BEARINGS

You're getting to know a lot
about the world around you,
from plants to animals to facts
about Earth. Keep exploring the
wild world around you!

100–149

A TRUE GLOBETROTTER

You are a natural explorer
who is tuned in to the world.
When nature calls, you know
the answer. Keep it up, and
they may be naming
mountains after you one day!

Sports Challenge

1. d
2. a
3. **False.** The first Olympic champion was a
   Greek cook named Coroebus, who won a
   sprint race in 776 B.C.E.
4. b
5. c
6. d
7. b
8. c
9. d
10. b

1. **True.** There is a reference in the
   household accounts of King Edward I in
   1300 of a cricket-like game being
   played in England.

2. **True.** William G. Morgan invented
   volleyball in 1895 for members of a YMCA,
   blending elements of several sports but
   without the physical contact.
3. **False.** John Newbery wrote a children's
   book that mentioned "base-ball" but did
   not give much description of the rules.
4. **False.** NASCAR stands for National
   Association for Stock Car Auto Racing.
5. **False.** Horseracing, including bareback
   races and chariot races, were part of
   the ancient Olympic Games of Greece
   beginning around 700 B.C.E.
6. **False.** American football originated by
   combining the rules of rugby and soccer.
7. **True.** It wasn't until a few years later
   that they cut holes in the bottom of the
   baskets to let the ball fall through.
8. **False.** Soccer was originally called
   association football. *Soccer* is derived
   from the second syllable of the word
   "association."
9. **True.** The earliest skis were discovered
   in Russia.
10. **False.** The sport is named after Rugby
    School in England, where the first rules
    were developed.
11. **False.** Although Napoleon did skate,
    organized skating competitions did not
    begin until more than 40 years after his
    death.

12. **True.** Missionaries sent to the island did
    not approve of the sport because men
    and women participated in it together.
13. **True.** The Mi'kmaq (Micmac) people of
    Canada played a hockey-like game in the
    1800s that was influenced by the Irish
    game of hurling.
14. **True.** In 1909 the rules were changed, and
    field goals were changed to three points.
15. **True.** Softball became known in the
    U.S.A. by many names, including "kitten
    ball," "mash ball," and "playground ball."
16. **True.** Nine pieces of stone, which were
    used as bowling pins, were found in the
    tomb of an Egyptian child buried
    around 3200 B.C.E.
17. **False.** The first skateboards appeared
    before Hawk was even born.
18. **True.** The winner of the first official
    cycling race held near Paris had to walk
    his bike up the steep hills.
19. **True.** This game was played in France in
    the 12th century.
20. **True.** James Naismith, the inventor of
    basketball, was born in Ontario, Canada,
    but he worked as a physical education
    director at Springfield College in
    Massachusetts, U.S.A.
21. **False.** Members of a curling team use
    brushes to help clean the ice in front of
    a sliding stone.

96-97, (main) Natursports/SS; 98, (br) homydesign/SS; 98, (cl) Michael Pettigrew/SS; 98, (cr) miqu77/SS; 98, (tl) Brocreative/SS; 99, (tr)
Andresr/SS; 99, (bl) Aspen Photo/SS; 100-101, (main) Natursports/SS; 102, (tr) Aaron M. Sprecher/Icon SMI/Corbis; 102, (br)
jcamilobernal/iS; 102, (cl) carroteater/SS; 103, (cl) Jerry Coli/Dreamstime; 103, (br) Sandra A. Dunlap/SS; 103, (tr) Bettmann/CORBIS;
104, (bl) Olga Besnard/Dreamstime; 104, (tr) Braverabbit/Dreamstime; 104, (br) Jamie Roach/SS; 105, (br) photoplanet.am/SS; 105, (cr)
Phil Sheldon/Popperfoto/GI; 105, (cl) versh/SS; **Making History [106-123]:** 106-107, (main) BARRY BISHOP/National Geographic Stock;
108, (tl) Eric Limon/SS; 108, (br) violetblue/SS; 109, (tl) Roberto A. Sanchez/iS; 109, (b-b) Michael Flippo/Dreamstime; 109, (b-c) Mike
Flippo/SS; 109, (b-d) sarnadex/iS; 109, (cr) Hank Shiffman/SS; 109, (b-a) H. Armstrong Roberts/ClassicStock/Corbis; 110-111, (main)

22. **True.** The Red Stockings organized in 1869 and toured the U.S.A. from New York to Oregon.

23. **True.** These strong-men helped popularize weightlifting in the 18th and 19th centuries.

24. **False.** Kung fu originated in China.

25. **False.** Skiers have been jumping for centuries.

26. **True.** Today, six players take the ice per team.

27. **True.** Basketballs, however, were too heavy, so a more appropriate volleyball was designed.

28. **False.** It was called lawn tennis, and today in Britain the sport is still formally known by that name.

29. **True.** Racing in downtown Louisville dates to at least 1783. The first racetrack opened in 1875.

30. **True.** These games often lasted several days and involved as many as 1,000 players on each team.

Map Mania!
Fields of Dreams,
pages 90–91

1. a
2. d
3. **True.** Each of the four screens on the video board is 72 feet high (22 m) and 160 feet wide (49 m), making for one heavy scoreboard!
4. c
5. a
6. d
7. b
8. Ski Dubai, **C—Dubai, United Arab Emirates**
9. Cowboys Stadium, **G—Dallas, Texas, U.S.A.**
10. Roman Colosseum, **A—Rome, Italy**
11. Wimbledon, **F—London, England**
12. Stadio Hernando Siles, **D—La Paz, Bolivia**
13. Rungrado May Day Stadium, **B—Pyongyang, North Korea**
14. Churchill Downs, **E—Louisville, Kentucky, U.S.A.**

From Champ
to Celebrity,
pages 92–93

1. a
2. c
3. **False.** In 2012 he was the seventh-richest soccer player in the world.
4. d
5. b
6. b
7. a
8. **False.** O'Neal played a rapping genie in the title role of the movie *Kazaam*.

9. c
10. b
11. **True.** LeBron James was the first overall draft pick in 2003 and that same year he signed a contract with Nike.
12. c

Record Setters,
pages 94–95

1. b
2. d
3. b
4. c
5. d
6. a
7. b
8. b
9. c

Fast, Furious, and Fun!
pages 96–97

1. b
2. **False.** Formula One is the most popular car racing series, viewed by millions of people in nearly 200 countries.
3. c
4. d
5. **False.** "Formula" refers to the set of racing rules that all teams and drivers agree to follow.
6. c
7. d
8. a
9. c
10. d
11. b

Gear and Garb,
pages 98–99

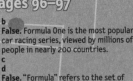

1. b
2. a
3. **True.** Goalies wear and use additional pads and equipment for protection and performance when playing "between the pipes."
4. a
5. d
6. c
7. c
8. b
9. **True.** In 1929, both the St. Louis Cardinals and New York Yankees placed numbers on the backs of their players to correspond to the order in which they batted.
10. d
11. c

The Soccer Scene,
pages 100–101

1. b
2. **False.** A player penalized with a red card is ejected from the match and cannot return.
3. d

4. c
5. d
6. **True.** Players who are not goalkeepers are penalized if they handle the ball.
7. d
8. a
9. c
10. b
11. a
12. d

Quest for Glory,
pages 102–103

1. d
2. c
3. b
4. a
5. **True.** Pickles discovered the stolen trophy several days later during a walk in south London with his owner.
6. b
7. **False.** The Boston Celtics won eight straight NBA titles, the most in the four major sports.
8. c
9. **True.** Both the players and staff get to spend a day with the trophy.
10. d
11. b

Game Show: Ultimate
Sports Challenge,
pages 104–105

1. c
2. c
3. **True.** The America's Cup is a trophy awarded to the winners of an international sailing competition of the same name that started in 1851.
4. b
5. a
6. **False.** The sport is called figure skating because skaters originally carved figures or patterns in the ice with their skates.
7. a
8. c
9. a
10. **False.** Snooker is a type of billiards, or pool.
11. d
12. a
13. c
14. b
15. Cristiano Ronaldo is a Portuguese soccer player who plays for Real Madrid in Spain.

Yuri Arcurs Media/SuperStock; 112, (tl) Lauri Patterson/IS; 112, (br) JeniFoto/SS; 113, (bl) Zastolskiy Victor/SS; 113, (cr) Nikin7d/SS; 113, (tl) Goran Bogicevic/SS; 114, (cl) Iakov Kalinin/SS; 114, (bl) Pius Lee/SS; 114, (tr) Chester Tugwell/SS; 115, (br) Dan Breckwoldt/SS; 115, (tr) Vladitto/SS; 115-116, (c) PILart/SS; 116, (cr) Hung Chung Chih/SS; 116, (tl) ivanastar/iS; 116, (bl) EdStock/iS, 116 (cr) EdStock/iS; 117, (bl) Debby Wong/SS; 117, (tr) AF archive/Alamy; 120-121, (main) ermess/SS; 122, (bcl) Arthur Hidden/SS; 122, (cl) craftvision/iS; 122, (tr) Daniel Korzeniewski/SS; 123, (br) Neftali/SS; 123, (cr) Ruigouveia/Dreamstime; 123, (cl) miteemaus5/iS; **Play With Your Food [124-143]:** 124-125, (main) Fenykepez/iS; 124-125, (main) Twin Design/SS; 124-125, (main) Derter/SS; 126-127, (main) Ostancov Vladislav/SS; 128, (br) huronphoto/iS; 128, (tl) Maks Narodenko/SS; 128, (cr)

SCORING

ROOKIE

You've got some catching up to do! Try flexing that mind and those muscles. Take a look around at the wide world of sports and find one that gets your heart and head racing. Then, get up and give it a shot. Remember: Some of the best athletes start slow but finish strong. Keep working and practicing, and you'll be a champion in all you do.

MINOR LEAGUE

You are a can't-miss prospect. You're not at the top of the podium just yet, but you've got the skills to get there. Read, watch, and discover. You can learn a lot from the world's top athletes. But don't get discouraged. Even the best have a setback once in a while. Lace up the sneakers, put on the gear, and train a bit more.

IN THE BIG LEAGUES

You, my friend, are at the top of you game! You've got speed, quick reflexes, and a sharp mind. You've probably memorized sports stats and the names of the world's top athletes. Top batting averages. Mos goals. Fastest times. No problem. Confidence is good, but don't get overconfident. There may be someone gaining on you. Push yourself to become the best *you* ca be, and you'll always be number one

Making History

Fashion Forward, pages 108–109

1. c
2. d
3. d
4. b
5. a
6. **False.** All Roman citizens were required to wear togas to gladiatorial games, weddings, and official ceremonies.
7. c
8. d
9. c
10. **True.** The wigs are used only during important ceremonies today.
11. c
12. a

New in the 1990s, pages 110–111

1. b
2. **True.** Lt. Col. Eileen Collins took the shuttle for a spin in February 1995.
3. **True.** The kid rap group Kriss Kross popularized the style.
4. c
5. d
6. c
7. a

8. b
9. a
10. **False.** Will Smith was the star.
11. b

Powers of Nature, pages 112–113

1. a
2. b
3. c
4. b
5. b
6. a
7. c
8. b
9. b
10. **False.** The storm lasted for four days.
11. c

Map Mania! Still Standing, pages 114–115

1. a
2. **True.** The Eiffel Tower was built for the 1889 World's Fair.
3. b
4. **True.** The tower started leaning as workers built the third story.
5. c
6. b

7. b
8. Big Ben, **E—London, England**
9. Eiffel Tower, **D—Paris, France**
10. The Sphinx, **A—Giza, Egypt**
11. Leaning Tower of Pisa, **C—Pisa, Italy**
12. The Kremlin, **G—Moscow, Russia**
13. Forbidden City, **B—Beijing, China**
14. Blarney Castle, **F—Blarney, Ireland**

Trends for the 2000s, pages 116–117

1. b
2. b
3. b
4. **True.** Obama's father originally came from Kenya.
5. b
6. **True.** *Atlantis* was the last shuttle to be used in a mission to space.
7. c
8. c
9. **False.** The Prius was sold in Japan in 1998. However, it made its North American debut in 2000.
10. a
11. b
12. a

American Pioneers, pages 118–119

1. **True.** There wasn't "toilet paper" because toilets hadn't been invented

urbanlight/SS; 129, (br) C.S. Lewis Pte. Ltd. 2004, reprinted by permission; 129, (tr) AF archive/Alamy; 129, (cl) llaszlo/SS; 130-131, (main) kitty/SS; 132, (tc) bonchan/SS; 132, (bc) Darla Hallmark/SS; 132, (c) Anders Stoustrup/SS; 133, (tc) hjschneider/SS; 133, (cr) matka_Wariatka/SS; 133, (b) Sarah Van Der Heijden/Dreamstime; 136-137, (main) monticello/SS; 138, (cl) successo/SS; 138, (tr) Satel22/Dreamstime; 138, (br) Amstockphoto/Dreamstime; 139, (br) Trudywsimmons/Dreamstime; 139, (cl) Linn Currie/SS; 140-141, (main) Brian Chase/SS; 142, (tr) Cuson/SS; 142, (cl) Tatyana Vyc/SS; 143, (b-a) arigato/SS; 143, (cl) Hlphoto/Dreamstime; 143, (b-b) Nattika/SS; 143, (cr) Martin Fowler/SS; 143, (t) FAUP/SS; 143, (b-d) Glenn Price/SS; 143, (b-c) leungchopan/SS; 143, (tcr) Boykov/SS; **The Numbers Game [144-163]:** 144-145, (main) SantiPhotoSS/SS; 146, (tr) Tim Laman/National Geographic Society/Corbis; 146, (b-c) Max

yet, but rags did the same job.
2. **True.** The Gold Rush saw lots of would-be miners head west to strike it rich.
3. **True.** The dog was named Seaman and is mentioned frequently in the trip journals.
4. **True.** People often slipped while getting in or out of wagons, falling under the wheels.
5. **False.** A wagon cost about $30.00.
6. **True.** Common food items included flour and coffee.
7. **False.** They did use grease made from beef fat, though.
8. **True.** Sometimes pioneers brought too much with them and had to abandon heavy things on the road.
9. **True.** Then, just like now, chocolate was a fantastic treat.
10. **True.** The wagons were spacious, allowing a family to travel with many belongings.
11. **True.** Riders could go through several horses before reaching their destination.
12. **False.** Most were farmers.
13. **True.** The dung was dry enough to catch fire.
14. **False.** Native Americans were among the least of the concerns of pioneers traveling west.
15. **False.** Most wagons were pulled by oxen.
16. **False.** Pioneer families often lived in one-room houses.
17. **False.** Baseball was invented in England.
18. **True.** Some places would have many different messages waiting for travelers.
19. **True.** This allowed wagons and animals to pack down the dirt of the graves so that wolves wouldn't find them.
20. **True.** A woman named Sacagawea was particularly helpful.

21. **True.** Traveling light meant the travelers could move quickly.
22. **False.** Sheep and cow fat was used for candles.
23. **True.** The man who shot him was a one-eyed explorer named Cruzatte.
24. **False.** The journey took between four and six months.
25. **False.** They collected bones to trade for supplies, and the bones were ground up to make fertilizer.
26. **False.** They were about 6 or 7 feet (1.8 to 2.1 m) high.
27. **False.** A wagon train traveled about 20 miles (32.1 km) a day.
28. **True.** Children were needed to help with farming, so they worked during the rest of the year.
29. **False.** Pioneers sometimes got salt from boiling down salty water until the water was all gone.
30. **True.** You can also play a video game that re-creates the trip.

Middle Ages Mayhem, pages 120–121

1. **True.** Farm animals, including cows, slept in the house with people.
2. c
3. c
4. a
5. c
6. b
7. b
8. **True.** Mice were sometimes taken to court for stealing part of a harvest.
9. d
10. b

ANSWERS

Game Show: Ultimate History Challenge, pages 122–123

1. c
2. c
3. b
4. a
5. **True.** Jeff Bezos, founder of Amazon.com, started the company from his home in Bellevue, Washington.
6. a
7. d
8. a
9. b
10. **True.** Called "pleasure gardens," they had fireworks, dancing, and some rides.
11. **True.** The social media site was used by students in college for years before the rest of the world was allowed to join.
12. b
13. d
14. **True.** The meal included 140 hogs, 14 oxen, 12 boars, and 6,000 pounds (2,721 kg) of venison.
15. Buffalo Bill Cody

SCORING

0–38

BLASTED BY THE PAST

You're not an expert historian because you live in the now. If you are curious about the past, you might want to read some books and do some searching on the World Wide Web to find out more about all the amazing things and people who were around before.

39–76

TERRIFIC WITH TIME

You know quite a few things about history and the people who made it. You like to fill your head with names, dates, and factoids. Keep it up, and they may be writing books about you one day.

77–115

THE GREATEST OF ALL TIME

Your brain is an encyclopedia of history! You're in the know for yesterday and today and have a very sharp mind. Use it to make connections between the past and the present. You're sure to make history!

Earey/SS; 146, (b-a) Darren Brode/SS; 146, (b-b) Car Culture/Corbis 60/Car Culture/Corbis; 146, (b-c) Darren Brode/SS; 146, (cr) Andre Coetzer/SS; 146, (tl) Warren Wimmer/Icon SMI/Corbis; 147, (tr) javarman/SS; 147, (br) AntonBalazh/SS; 150-151, (main) Lou Jones/Lonely Planet Images/GI; 152-153, (main) Petrenko Andriy/SS; 154- 155, (main) clearviewstock/SS; 156, (tr) Pictorial Press Ltd/Alamy; 156, (cl) Nomad_Soul/SS; 156, (br) Pablo Rogat/SS; 157, (tr) Welland Lau/SS; 157, (br) Tatiana Popova/SS; 157, (cr) Dimedrol68/SS; 157, (cr) images.etc/SS; 158-159, (main) YK/SS; 160, (tcr) Rick Becker-Leckrone/SS; 160, (tl) PinkTag/iS; 160- 161, (c) BryanToro/iS; 161, (tr) Mombo76/Dreamstime; 161, (br) Guy J. Sagi/SS; 162, (cr) RGB Ventures LLC dba SuperStock/Alamy; 162, (cl) Generistock/iS; 163, (cr) Sebastian Kaulitzki/Alamy; 163, (br) Hayley Louize Ballard/Alamy; 163, (cl) Igor Bulgarin/SS; **Answer Key [164-176]:** 164, (tc) Eric

PLAY WITH YOUR FOOD

Eat My Words!
pages 126–127

1. a
2. b
3. a
4. b
5. d
6. **False.** The classic tale by Judi Barrett takes place in a tiny town called Chewandswallow.
7. **True.** The French stew ratatouille is usually made with tomatoes, garlic, onions, zucchini, eggplant, peppers, and a mixture of tasty herbs.
8. d
9. d
10. c
11. **False.** She gives Edmund his favorite food, a sweet treat known as Turkish Delight.

Mind Your Manners,
pages 128–129

1. a
2. a
3. **True.** It resembles incense burning, symbolizing offering food for the dead.
4. b
5. d
6. b
7. d
8. c
9. **False.** Slurping is considered an acceptable and enjoyable way to eat soup in Japan.
10. b
11. d

Snacks From the Sea,
pages 130–131

1. **True.** More than 170 billion pounds (77.9 million metric tons) of seafood are caught each year.
2. c
3. a
4. b
5. **True.** Shrimp, salmon, and oysters are some of the seafood that is farmed.
6. b
7. a
8. d
9. **True.** It was bought jointly by owners of a restaurant in Hong Kong and a chain of sushi bars.
10. c

Map Mania! Global Grub,
pages 132–133

1. **True.** In Greece, a similar skewered food is prepared called souvlaki.
2. d
3. c
4. b
5. a
6. **False.** There is no rabbit in bunny chow.

Originally these spicy bread bowls were vegetarian, but later versions added mutton, lamb, or chicken.
7. Turkey, **D**
8. Iceland, **C**
9. Mexico, **E**
10. Germany, **B**
11. Australia, **F**
12. South Africa, **A**

Extreme Eats,
pages 134–135

1. **True.** The sculpture was dumped into a special pit that turns waste into energy.
2. **False.** *Theobroma's* literal translation is "food of the gods."
3. **True.** In order not to be wasteful of food, the "cream" pies were actually shaving cream!
4. **True.** The fruit is pungent, with some people saying it smells like dirty socks and bad cheese.
5. **True.** Janet Harris ate each of the 7,175 peas one by one using chopsticks!
6. **False.** People throw tomatoes. The tomatoes have to be crushed first to avoid injuries.
7. **False.** In 2003, a man in India swallowed 200 earthworms measuring at least 4 inches (10 cm) in 30 seconds.
8. **False.** In addition to burgers, snake meat is used in soups, shish kebabs, and even beverages.
9. **True.** Hoping to put an end to worldwide famine, the United Nations is actively promoting edible insects as a sustainable food source.
10. **True.** Canstruction's goal is to bring awareness to hunger issues around the world. The canned food is donated to local food banks.
11. **False.** Joey "Jaws" Chestnut actually ate a record 266 dumplings!
12. **True.** If you are squeamish about eating live maggots, you can put the cheese in a sealed bag until they die.
13. **False.** Juckes completed the race in 3 hours 47 minutes 15 seconds dressed as a carrot.
14. **True.** The 12-inch pizzas were made by Great Kitchens and delivered on July 4, 2012, just in time for Independence Day.
15. **False.** Roast Ox–flavored potato chips can be found in England.
16. **False.** The pomelo is a gift given during Chinese New Year's and is a symbol of prosperity and good luck.
17. **True.** The dandelion is used in fresh salads or sometimes sautéed in oil. It's packed with Vitamin K.
18. **False.** A quahog is a hard-shelled clam found in the waters off Cape Cod in the United States.
19. **True.** The restaurant is located in an abandoned limestone mine.
20. **True.** Robots take orders, deliver meals, prepare omelets, and even flip burgers!
21. **False.** Juice from the prickly pear cactus is filled with nutrients.
22. **True.** The inventor of Soylent claims that the liquid has all the nutrition that humans need to live.
23. **True.** India's Naga king chili is the hottest known pepper in the world.

24. **True.** Part of a conservation area for birds, the vulture restaurant is a drop-off site for roadkill, butcher shop remains, and the carcasses of dead farm animals.
25. **False.** Bird saliva is the primary ingredient in the soup that has been prized in China for its health benefits for more than 1,000 years.
26. **False.** Beef-tongue ice cream is popular in Japan. Other unusual flavors include eel, raw horse, curry, crab, and octopus.
27. **True.** The sticky flood pushed buildings off their foundations and killed 21 people.
28. **False.** Food photographers use dish soap and many other unappetizing tricks to make food look tasty for the camera.
29. **True.** The gilded sweet was auctioned off at $1,600, and the money was donated to charity.
30. **False.** The *roo* is actually kangaroo, and it's the most popular pizza on the menu.

Grow Your Groceries,
pages 136–137

1. b
2. **True.** Cultures around the world have used natural dyes to add color to their clothing and household items and even to decorate their bodies!
3. d
4. b
5. d
6. a
7. c
8. c
9. c
10. b
11. **False.** It comes from the Narragansett Native American word *askutasquash,* which means "eaten raw."
12. b

Street Food,
pages 138–139

1. b
2. c
3. d
4. b
5. a
6. d
7. a
8. **True.** Tarantulas are considered a local delicacy and are sometimes enjoyed sprinkled with soy sauce.
9. a
10. **True.** Head to downtown Anchorage to sample Alaska's best reindeer dogs with all the toppings. Just don't tell Santa!
11. b

Sweet Treats,
pages 140–141

1. b
2. **True.** Beekeepers were stumped by the colorful honey until their investigation found the bees feasting on the colored candy shells.
3. d
4. c

Isselee /SS; 164, (bl) kyokoliberty/SS; 165, (tr) WilleeCole/SS; 166, (tc) Robert Mandel/SS; 166, (tr) StudioSmart/SS; 166, (cr) Paul Orr/SS; 166, (cl) dutourdumonde/SS; 167, (l) Catherine Lane/iS; 167, (bcl) Scott O'Dell/Houghton Mifflin Harcourt; 168, (bc) Eric Isselee/SS; 168, (tr) RJAce1014/SS; 168, (tl) Cindy Ord/GI Entertainment /GI; 168, (c) Richard Harbaugh/Disney ABC Television Group/GI; 168, (br) Wong Hock weng/SS; 169, (cr) NASA and The Hubble Heritage Team/NASA; 170, (tr) Dennis Donohue/SS; 171, (bl) Celso Pupo rodrigues/Dreamstime; 171, (c) Andresr/SS; 171, (br) Braverabbit/Dreamstime; 171, (bc) tkachuk/SS; 171, (tc) Jianbinglee/Dreamstime; 172, (bc) Chester Tugwell/SS; 172, (cl) violetblue/SS; 172, (c) JeniFoto/SS; 173, (tr) Neftali/SS; 174, (t) llaszlo/SS; 174, (cr) Linn Currie/SS; 175, (bl) javarman/SS; 176, (c) Pablo Rogat/SS; 176, (cl) Petrenko Andriy/SS; 176, (tr) Mombo76/Dreamstime; 176, (cr) Igor Bulgarin/SS

5. c
6. b
7. **True.** The smells from the Krispy Kreme bakery in Winston-Salem, North Carolina, U.S.A., were so delicious to neighbors they wanted to buy right from the sidewalk.
8. d
9. **True.** White chocolate is made from cocoa butter, sugar, and vanilla and is actually not chocolate.
10. a
11. b

Game Show: Ultimate Food Challenge, pages 142–143

1. a
2. b
3. d
4. d
5. c
6. b
7. **True.** Removing moisture dries out the food and slows the rate at which it spoils.
8. b
9. a

10. **False.** They were extremely successful, developing techniques of finding vegetables and grain that thrived at high altitudes and creating stone terraces to increase the amount of flat land for crops.
11. a
12. a
13. b
14. **False.** This delicious pie found in the region of the United States called Pennsylvania Dutch Country has sweet molasses in it, but no flies!
15. a

SCORING

0–40

FOOD FOR THOUGHT
Food facts are probably not your idea of fabulous fun, but some of life's most delicious discoveries are found on our plates. We learn a lot about our world and ourselves by understanding more about what we eat. Open your mind and mouth to the food around you.

41–81

SOMETHING TO CHEW ON
Your food knowledge is a buffet of facts and insights. You take a bite out of life and savor the world around you. Keep feeding yourself facts and digesting the information to become a true expert on all things edible.

82–123

A BANQUET OF KNOWLEDGE
When it comes to tasty trivia, you feast like royalty. Whether it's fried, boiled, pickled, or baked, you've got the dish on food. Keep drinking in the food facts around you, and, who knows, one day they may even name a dessert after you. Sweet!

The Numbers Game

Think Fast! pages 146–147

1. c
2. b
3. b
4. d
5. c
6. a
7. a
8. **True.** The crew of the Apollo 10 spacecraft reentered Earth's atmosphere at this speed.
9. c
10. b
11. d

True or False? Freaky Figures, pages 148–149

1. **False.** Jason Schayot once spit a seed 78.5 feet (23.9 m).
2. **True.** Jackie Bibby, the "Snake Man," also set a record for most rattlesnakes held at once in his mouth.

3. **False.** The previous record of 40 skips was broken by a Pennsylvania man who tossed a stone across the water for 51 skips.
4. **False.** Brown recluse spiders can have only about 150 spiderlings a year. That's still a lot of spiders.
5. **True.** The world's largest chocolate bar weighed 12,190 pounds (5,529 kg), about the weight of an Asian elephant.
6. **True.** The catfish was roughly the size of a grizzly bear.
7. **True.** Julian Pavone recorded the CD "Go, Baby" with bassist Ralphe Armstrong.
8. **False.** That was the length of Ram Singh Chauhan's mustache as of 2013 after growing it for 42 years.
9. **True.** It took 15 hours, and they performed this feat to raise money for the Royal Marine Association in England.
10. **True.** Tran Van Hay had hair that measured 18.4 feet (5.6 m). He didn't cut his hair for 50 years.
11. **True.** Andriy Kostash did all those push-ups in less than 3 hours.
12. **False.** The world record is only 18.1 seconds.
13. **False.** "B-Girl Spinderella" did a continuous head spin in break-dancing for an incredible 13 minutes 53 seconds when she was 11 years old.
14. **True.** Naomi Kutin lifted more than twice her own weight to set the record.

15. **True.** All the hens in the United States produce a total of 92.9 billion eggs yearly.
16. **False.** The people dressed up as Superman.
17. **False.** A person's shout can be as loud as a car horn at 110 decibels, but a siren is slightly louder at 120 decibels.
18. **True.** In 1993, Ashrita Furman climbed up to the snow-line of Mount Fuji one pogo hop at a time.
19. **False.** Tamae Watanabe climbed Mount Everest when she was 73 years old.
20. **True.** Many of the bees had their stingers removed by hand.
21. **True.** Ashish Sharma of India spent 120 hours 23 minutes glued to a TV. That's a lot of commercials!
22. **True.** Find a deck of cards and see for yourself.
23. **False.** The sandwich was actually 10 times the size at 2,411 feet (735 m). Three teams in Lebanon made the sandwich in 2011.
24. **True.** It included edible gold flakes and was served at a restaurant called Serendipity 3 in New York City.
25. **True.** He rode the Ferris wheel for 48 hours.
26. **True.** A professional surfer from Hawaii surfed the wave in Nazare, Portugal.
27. **True.** Like all rodents' teeth, a rabbit's front teeth are constantly growing.

175

28. **True.** It was a seafood stew.
29. **False.** Around 400 people in the U.S. survive lightning strikes each year.
30. **True.** About 2,500 teachers teach those students at the City Montessori School in Lucknow, India.

Pick a Number ... pages 150–151

1. a
2. c
3. b
4. **True.** Also, when you write out the numerals 0–10, the letter "e" occurs ten times.
5. a
6. **False.** It equals 100.
7. a
8. a
9. **True.** So the total number of dots is 21.
10. c
11. d

The Amazing Human Machine, pages 152–153

1. c
2. c
3. b
4. a
5. a
6. a
7. c
8. b
9. **False.** Tiny eight-legged mites are always living in your eyelashes.
10. c
11. a
12. b

To Infinity ... and Beyond! pages 154–155

1. a
2. b
3. d

4. d
5. c
6. c
7. **Gross but true.** The urine is passed through a recycling system on the station.
8. c
9. c
10. d
11. a
12. b

By the Numbers, pages 156–157

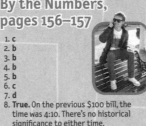

1. c
2. b
3. b
4. b
5. b
6. c
7. d
8. **True.** On the previous $100 bill, the time was 4:10. There's no historical significance to either time.
9. d
10. d
11. c
12. c

Wonders of Nature, pages 158–159

1. b
2. c
3. a
4. a
5. d
6. **True.** The eel can produce an electric shock with about as much energy (500 watts) as five lightbulbs.
7. c
8. **True.** Some seals living in the Arctic can hold their breath for an hour or more under the ice.
9. c
10. d
11. a
12. d

That's Entertainment! pages 160–161

1. c
2. a
3. d
4. b
5. c
6. b
7. **True.** There are records for most hours of playing Monopoly in a bathtub, in a tree, and in other crazy places.
8. a
9. a
10. c
11. a

Game Show: Ultimate Numbers Challenge, pages 162–163

1. d
2. **False.** The average person speaks 31,500 words per day.
3. **True.** Neil Armstrong took manual control of the spacecraft and landed with only about 30 seconds of fuel to spare.
4. c
5. a
6. c
7. b
8. c
9. **True.** And everyone has his or her own unique combination of bacteria, like a gross fingerprint.
10. b
11. c
12. c
13. c
14. c
15. Candy Crush

SCORING

0–41

NUMB TO NUMBERS
Digits don't do it for you, but that's okay. Just remember, almost everything relies on math and measurements, so count on needing to count someday.

42–84

COOL AS CALCULATOR
For you, most numbers are as easy as 1, 2, 3. You "even" know a few "odd" facts about a number of things. Keep adding answers to your brain to multiply your knowledge.

85–126

MATHEMAGICIAN!
When it comes to numbers, your knowledge is almost infinite. How does it feel to be a walking computer?